D0548406

THE
LITTLE
BOOK
OF
WELSH
LANDMARKS

MARK REES

The
History
Press

First published 2018

The History Press
The Mill, Brimscombe Port
Stroud, Gloucestershire, GL5 2QG
www.thehistorypress.co.uk

British Library Cataloguing in Publication Data.
A catalogue record for this book is available from the British Library.

ISBN 978 0 7509 8905 3

Typesetting and origination by The History Press
Printed and bound in Great Britain by TJ International Ltd

Front cover image: View from Devil's Pulpit to Tintern Abbey. © Nessy-
Pic (Wikimedia, CC BY-SA 4.0)

CONTENTS

About the Author   4

Acknowledgements   5

Introduction   7

1 Areas of Outstanding Natural Beauty   9

2 Wonders of the World   21

3 The Seven Wonders of Wales   31

4 Climbing the Highest Peaks   37

5 Getting Back to Nature   51

6 Coastal Treasures   69

7 A Land of Castles   91

8 Spectacular Spans   113

9 Living in Style   123

10 Religious Miracles   145

11 Forged by History   175

ABOUT THE AUTHOR

For more than fifteen years, Mark Rees has published articles about the arts and culture in some of Wales' best-selling newspapers and magazines. His roles have included arts editor for the South Wales Evening Post, and what's on editor for the Carmarthen Journal, Llanelli Star and Swansea Life. His previous books for The History Press include The Little Book of Welsh Culture (2016) and Ghosts of Wales: Accounts from the Victorian Archives (2017).

ACKNOWLEDGEMENTS

I would like to thank everyone who has helped me on my journey in search of Wales' finest landmarks. In particular, a huge diolch o'r galon to my family for supporting me on yet another crazy writing adventure, and to Nicola Guy and everyone at The History Press for commissioning the book which you now hold in your hands.

A collection of this nature would not have been possible without some incredible photography, and all of the photographers have been individually credited throughout.

Several people suggested landmarks which I might have overlooked otherwise. Those whose favourites have been included are: Jason Evans, Laura Grove, Rory Castle Jones and Chris Peregrine.

Finally, in no particular order, my thanks go to: Emma Hardy and Bolly the cat; Kev Johns; Chris Carra; Owen Staton; Tim Batcup and all at Cover to Cover bookshop; Mal Pope; Wyn Thomas; Simon Davies and all at The Comix Shoppe; Ian Parsons; Peter Richards and all at Fluellen Theatre Company; Adrian White; and to my football-watching companions Jean and Lindsay.

INTRODUCTION

When I first began to write a 'little book' of Wales's greatest landmarks, it seemed like the easiest job in the world. I mean, anyone who lives in Cymru will know that all you have to do to find a landmark is to walk out out of your front door, and there they are. Look up or down, left or right, and you'll see towering mountains, glistening rivers, miraculous churches and prehistoric monuments stretching for as far as the eye can see.

But therein lies the problem.

I discovered very early on that there are so many potential landmarks in God's own country that whittling down the thousands on offer to just a measly few hundred would be a monumental task.

If I had included every landmark on my original longlist, this book would more resemble an encyclopaedia – and I'd still be writing it right now.

To put things into perspective, there are said to be around 600 castles in Wales alone, with around 100 of them still standing. That means I could have written about nothing but castles, and still only covered around 50 per cent of them before hitting my word count.

The only way to put some kind of order on things was to decide upon a selection process. To begin with, I ticked off all of the 'big hitters' which are covered in the first two chapters, the world-class wonders which have, quite rightly, been declared UNESCO World Heritage Sites and Areas of Outstanding Natural Beauty.

But with the likes of Snowdonia, the Gower Peninsula and the Brecon Beacons done and dusted, what next? It was important to include a wide selection of landmarks from all across Wales, and in order to strike a balance I divided this book into eleven roughly equal-sized chapters, ranging from stately homes to neolithic megaliths.

Next, each of the places included had to have a uniqueness about them to elevate them above the crowd. This could be something simple, like an amazing view or an idyllic beauty spot, to something a bit more complex, like a convoluted history intertwined with wars, myths and legends.

This process worked well, but it did present me with one unique problem – many of the landmarks could quite easily have been included in multiple chapters. For example, eagle-eyed readers might notice that the beaches of Gower are strangely absent from the chapter about coastal landmarks; they can instead found in the earlier chapter about Wales's Areas of Outstanding Natural Beauty. Or that The Castles and Town Walls of King Edward in Gwynedd are nowhere to be seen in the castles chapter; they can instead be found in the UNESCO World Heritage Sites section. While this isn't ideal, the only alternative would have been to repeat information which, in a volume of this size, would have been something of a luxury.

Ultimately, this book does not claim or pretend to be a comprehensive guide to every landmark in Wales. Rather, it is intended to serve as a tantalising teaser to the treasures on offer, and one which will whet your appetite enough to inspire you to head off on a cultural adventure of your own.

I hope that you enjoy reading this collection as much as I enjoyed writing it, and even if some of the locations are already familiar to you, maybe you'll learn something new and pick up some bits of trivia along the way.

If you are lucky enough to live in Wales, or are planning on visiting in the future, you can be certain of one thing: there are thousands of landmarks out there to explore, and many of them will be right on your doorstep.

Mark Rees, 2018

A NOTE ON THE TEXT

Most of the landmarks in this book are now commonly known by either their Welsh or English names. In some cases they might be known by both, or maybe an Anglicisation of the original Welsh name. I have used the most common place names and spelling throughout, and supplied Welsh and English translations where appropriate.

1

AREAS OF OUTSTANDING NATURAL BEAUTY

In 1956, the Gower Peninsula became the United Kingdom's first Area of Outstanding Natural Beauty (AONB). Singled out for special conservation, it has since been joined by four others in Wales: Anglesey, the Clwydian Range and Dee Valley, the Llŷn Peninsula, and the Wye Valley, which partially crosses over the border into England.

Each beauty spot is unique; they were selected for a multitude of reasons, including the importance of their landscape, their ancient history, the surrounding area's culture and heritage, their ecology and prominence of rare plants and animals, and in all five cases, their sheer good looks.

AONBs in Wales are designated by the Welsh government body Natural Resources Wales, which was formed in 2013 following the merger of the Countryside Council for Wales, Environment Agency Wales, and the Forestry Commission Wales. The areas are all protected by law, and the aim is to enhance, as well as preserve, their features.

These mountains and valleys, islands and lakes, cover about 5 per cent of the land. And as well as representing some of the best that the country has to offer, they are also filled with even more landmarks within landmarks.

South Stack Lighthouse. © *Denis Egan (Wikimedia, CC BY 2.0)*

ANGLESEY

Anglesey – Ynys Môn in Welsh – received its AONB status in 1967.

Sitting just off the north-west of the country, it is Wales's largest island, covering 276 square miles of land. This makes it the largest island in the Irish Sea in terms of area, and second only to the Isle of Man in terms of population.

Its designated AONB area covers the vast majority of its coastline, approximately one third of the island. Its protected status not only preserves its existing treasures, but ensures that it won't be damaged by any unsuitable developments in the future.

Anglesey is accessible from the mainland by two bridges: the Menai Suspension Bridge and the Britannia Bridge, which are landmarks in their own right and feature later in this book. The location makes it a popular destination for sailors, surfers and anglers, and the best way to explore it is along the 125-mile Isle of Anglesey Coastal Path. Starting at St Cybi's Grade I listed medieval church in Holyhead, the county's largest town, the route takes in its many beaches, wich are backed by sand dunes and limestone cliffs.

When it comes to wildlife, there are many rare and threatened species on and around the island. Harbour porpoises can be seen in the water, the distinctive wings of the marsh fritillary butterflies in the air, while the rivers have seen the return of the otter.

The South Stack Cliffs, a Royal Society for the Protection of Birds (RSPB) nature reserve, is home to up to 9,000 birds, including puffins and choughs. The rare South Stack fleawort plant is also endemic to the cliffs, but tread carefully – it is also home to an adder or two.

Inland, the Dingle Nature Reserve in Llangefni is 25 acres of ancient woodland divided in two by the Afon Cefni river. There are sculptures to be found among the wildlife, and its Welsh name Nant y Pandy is derived from an old wool mill which was in the valley.

Wales is home to the UK's second-largest region of marshy fen area, which spans four nature reserves, three of which are in Anglesey. Collectively known as the Anglesey Fens, they are Cors Bodeilio, Cors Goch, and the largest of the trio, Cors Erddreiniog. The fourth, Cors Geirch, can be found in fellow AONB the Llŷn Peninsula.

There are three designated heritage coasts in Anglesey. Much like being designated an AONB, they are singled out for their importance by Natural Resources Wales for the benefit of the public who are free to explore and enjoy them.

North Anglesey is the island's longest heritage coast, a 17-mile stretch of beaches which begins at Church Bay, a pebble and sand beach dotted with rockpools, and heads east towards Dulas Bay, a small beach with an eye-catching shipwreck.

Highlights along the route include Cemlyn Bay and Lagoon, which hosts an important colony of tern seabirds, and Amlwch, Wales's most northerly town. Nearby Parys Mountain was home to Europe's largest copper mine in the eighteenth century.

On the island's south-west coast, the Aberffraw Bay heritage coast is a 4.5-mile trek around the giant sand dunes of Aberffraw Bay, some of which can reach as high as 10m. The walk starts in Aberffraw which, in the Middle Ages, was the capital of the Kingdom of Gwynedd.

A spectacular landmark nearby is the Grade II* listed church of Saint Cwyfan, which is quite appropriately known as the 'Church in the Sea'. Originally dating from the twelfth century, it stands on Cribinau, a tiny island cut off from the mainland following centuries of erosion, and is still used as a place of worship today in the summer months.

Other highlights include the fly-fishers' favourite lake of Llyn Coron, and the neolithic burial chamber Barclodiad y Gawres between Aberffraw and the village of Rhosneigr.

Finally, Anglesey's third heritage coast is an 8-mile route around Holy Island. It starts at Trearddur Bay, a popular bathing spot, taking in the must-visit South Stack as it winds its way towards the striking North Stack. There are numerous landmarks en route, from the island's iconic lighthouse to its large volume of ancient stones.

Holy Island is home to Holyhead Mountain, which slopes down into the Irish Sea and hosts a large number of breeding birds. With an elevation of 220m, it is the highest mountain in the county. The highest mountain on the island of Anglesey, and the county's second-highest mountain, is Mynydd Bodafon, with an elevation of 178m.

On a good day, the Emerald Isle can be seen across the waters from the peak of Holyhead Mountain, and the main route to Dublin by sea is from the port of Holyhead. The harbour's Victorian breakwater in Soldier's Point, is the longest of its kind in the UK. Snaking its way 1.7 miles out to sea, you can wind your way along its promenade to reach the Holyhead Breakwater Lighthouse.

Did You Know ...

Llanbadrig, the name of a village at the northern peak of Anglesey, translates as the Church of St Patrick. A church bearing the saint's name can be found near the village of Cemaes, and, according to the legend, the Irish saint was shipwrecked there in AD 440 as he attempted to cross the waters. Seeking refuge in Ogof Badrig (Patrick's Cave), he established a wooden church nearby, on the site of which the current church was built in the fourteenth century.

CLWYDIAN RANGE AND DEE VALLEY

The Clwydian Range and Dee Valley is the most recent addition to Wales's list of AONBs.

Eglywseg Mountain. © *Mattcymru2 (Wikimedia, CC BY-SA 3.0)*

Designated in 1985, the heather-clad 'gateway to north Wales' covers miles of tranquil open land and forestry, tracing the route of the River Dee from the seaside town of Prestatyn to the hills of Llangollen.

The boundaries of the AONB were greatly expanded in 2011, heading southwards to take in the Dee Valley. It now covers 150 square miles of land, and newer additions include the castles Castell Dinas Brân and Chirk Castle, the Pontcysyllte Aqueduct World Heritage Site, and Valle Crucis Abbey. Its summits offer views as far afield as the tips of Snowdonia in the west to the Peak District National Park in central England to the east. The AONB's highest point is Moel y Gamelin hill, a Marilyn north of Llangollen, which stands 577m tall.

At the top of Moel Famau (554m), which straddles the border between the counties of Denbighshire and Flintshire, is the Jubilee Tower. This unfinished obelisk was started in 1810 to mark the golden jubilee of George III, but much of it was destroyed by strong winds in 1862.

The history of the area can be traced back 400 million years, with ancient finds scattered across the landscape. Foel Fenlli hill, which has an elevation of 511m, has an Iron Age hill fort at its peak, as does fellow Marilyn Penycloddiau. One of the largest in the country, it covers 64 acres, and a burial mound and stone tools are among the Bronze Age discoveries that have been made there.

There are also plenty of legends in the area, and strong links with Arthurian mythology. The Maen Huail in the Denbighshire town of Ruthin is a limestone block with a plaque which reads: 'On this stone the legendary King Arthur beheaded Huail, brother of Gildas the historian, his rival in love and war.' In the Mold village of Loggerheads, Carreg Carn March Arthur (The Stone of Arthur's Steed) is said to bear the hoofprint of the legendary king's mare Llamrai. According to the story, it was created as they jumped from a cliff while fleeing from the Saxons. It is now protected by an arched boundary stone bearing a plaque.

Rocks bearing names such as Craig Arthur (Arthur's Rock) and Craig y Forwyn (Maiden's Crag) can be found in the Eglwyseg Valley, home to a 4.5 mile limestone escarpment which is popular with rock climbers. With a high point of 513m at Mynydd Eglwyseg, the World's End vale at the head of the valley offers panoramic views across the land.

The Horseshoe Pass mountain pass is a scenic route around the valley, which also leads to a rather unique landmark at its summit: the only cafe to be included in this book. The Ponderosa Cafe Complex is a remote place of sustenance, and is an almost compulsory stop or meeting place for many people exploring the range.

Did You Know ...

You can follow the Offa's Dyke National Trail, which leads along the Welsh and English border, all the way from one AONB in the north of Wales, the Clwydian Range and Dee Valley, to another in the south of Wales, the Wye Valley?

LLŶN PENINSULA

The Llŷn Peninsula is Wales's second-oldest AONB. Created in 1956, soon after the Gower Peninsula became the first

White Hall (centre) on Porthdinllaen Beach. © *PangolinOne*
(Wikimedia, CC BY-SA 4.0)

in the UK, it spans around 62 square miles, covering about a
quarter of the Gwynedd peninsula.

Surrounded on either side by the Irish Sea and Cardigan
Bay, with the ancient holy isle of Bardsey Island at its peak, the
AONB takes in most of the area's coast and hills. It is divided
into two sections: the southern part begins at the small offshore
island Carreg y Defaid, from where it curves around the coast
before moving inland; following a break near Morfa Nefyn, it
continues northward after the town of Nefyn.

It is in the north where the peninsula's highest peaks can be
found, with the likes of Bwlch Mawr and Gyrn Ddu rising more
than 500m. The tallest of them all is the three-peaked Yr Eifl,
and its central summit, Garn Ganol, reaches 561m.

One of the best ways to explore the peninsula is by following
the Llŷn Coastal Path, a 91-mile waymarked route which
has been integrated into the Wales Coast Path. It starts at
Caernarfon, and passes many a landmark, as well as a few
traditional kissing gates, as it leads the way to Porthmadog.

The beaches, such as seaside resort Abersoch, are very much
classical golden sweeps of bay. A go-to destination for watersports
aficionados, the peninsula was home to Wakestock for several
years, said to be 'Europe's largest wakeboarding festival'.

There are several National Trust attractions in the peninsula,
such as Llanbedrog, with its distinctive and brightly coloured
beach huts. A more secluded gem is Porthdinllaen, a small
fishing village within touching distance of the water.

When it comes to wildlife, grey seals and bottlenose dolphins can be seen off the coast, and there are many breeding spots for birds, such as the cove of Porth Meudwy, which is also a departure spot to see countless more on Bardsey Island.

Pen Llŷn a'r Sarnau in Cardigan Bay is a huge protected Special Area of Conservation (SAC), and is home to many marine habitats, plants, animals and shallow reefs. Extending down towards Aberystwyth, the first half of its name, Pen Llŷn, refers to the Llŷn Peninsula, while the second half, Sarnau, is the Welsh word for causeway, relating to a trio of reefs.

Another SAC and Site of Special Scientific Interest (SSSI) is Cors Geirch National Nature Reserve. In the spring, the marshy wetland between Nefyn and Pwllheli is awash with colour, coming alive with primroses and bluebells which attract winged insects such as the marsh fritillary butterfly, which can also be seen in Anglesey.

Did You Know …

Porthor, a secluded beach in the Llŷn Peninsula, is known as the 'whistling sands'. It is one of the few beaches in the world were the sands do actually 'whistle', with the sound created when the grains rub together.

GOWER PENINSULA

The Gower Peninsula is the UK's original AONB, and it's easy to see why. Singled out for its natural beauty in 1956, the peninsula just west of Swansea is 70 square miles of golden sands, archaeological wonders, protected geology and countless curiosities which can be explored along the 38-mile Wales Coast Path walk which circles around from Mumbles to Crofty.

Gower, or Gŵyr in Welsh, is probably best known globally for its beaches, and arguably the most famous of them all is Rhossili Bay. The largest beach on the peninsula, its 3 miles of white sand has claimed many an award over the years, including 'Best Beach in Europe' from *Suitcase* magazine. It even ruffled a few feathers in the southern hemisphere when the magazine also named it as

Rhossilli Worm's Head. © *tomyst (Wikimedia, CC BY 3.0)*

the ninth best beach in the world – edging out some of the more celebrated beaches Down Under in the process.

Its most distinctive, and photographed, landmark is Worm's Head, named by the Vikings for its resemblance to a dragon's head, with *wurm* being the Viking word for dragon. The rocky tidal island protrudes into the sea, and is connected to the mainland by a causeway. It can be crossed along the ominously named Devil's Bridge, a naturally formed bridge which leads towards the 'serpent's' head.

There are twenty-five beaches along the coastline in total, and many others are also award winners, and regularly receive Blue Flag awards, the gold standard for high-quality beaches. While a detailed look at every beach in Gower is beyond the scope of this book, they include Oxwich Bay, Gower's second-largest beach and a National Nature Reserve; the National Trust-owned Whiteford, with the vast Whiteford Sands; Port Eynon, which has a fascinating history of smugglers lurking in its caves, as do the more secluded areas like Brandy Cove and Pwll Du; Caswell Bay and Langland Bay, which are both surfing hotspots and popular tourist destinations, with the latter housing a long row of in-demand and well-known beach huts; and from a purely aesthetic point of view, the bay with the most picturesque panorama would probably be Three Cliffs Bay, a dramatic coastal landscape bordered by Pobbles Bay and Tor Bay.

Inland there are cliffs, farmland and more than eighty ancient scheduled monuments and sites, many of which are surrounded by myths, legends and ghost stories. On the 5-mile-long Cefn Bryn ridge is the neolithic burial ground Maen Ceti (Arthur's Stone). According to one variation of its origin, King Arthur himself was walking along the Carmarthenshire shore when he felt a pebble in his shoe. Removing it and hurling it across the estuary, it grew in size as it landed in its current spot opposite Reynoldston car park.

Another ancient landmark which is worth the extra effort to see, if not necessarily enter, is Paviland Cave. In the nineteenth century, an archaeological find of global significance was discovered by William Buckland, Professor of Geology at Oxford University, just inside the cave's entrance. Named 'The Red Lady of Paviland', it was a skeleton covered in a red ochre which had stained the bones, and which was mistakenly believed to be female, but was later confirmed to be male. Access to the cave, which is just 10m high and 7m wide, is often blocked by the tide.

Did You Know...

The Gower Peninsula is where the much-decorated composer Sir Karl Jenkins was born and raised. The first Welsh composer to receive a knighthood hails from the village of Penclawdd, which is also famous for its cockles.

WYE VALLEY

The Wye Valley, or Dyffryn Gwy in Welsh, has quite a claim to fame: it is credited with giving birth to British tourism in the eighteenth century. Tourists have flocked to its wild woodlands, limestone gorge and untamed waters for centuries, with some of the Romantic wanderers who paid a visit to draw inspiration

View from Devil's Pulpit to Tintern Abbey. © *Nessy-Pic (Wikimedia, CC BY-SA 4.0)*

for their words and works of art including Samuel Taylor Coleridge, William Gilpin, Thomas Gray, Alexander Pope, William Makepeace Thackeray, J.M.W. Turner and William Wordsworth.

The only AONB to extend across both Wales and England, the Wye Valley was designated in 1971, and its 128 square miles contain SSSIs, SACs, Scheduled Monuments and National Nature Reserves.

Flowing through the valley is the River Wye, the first complete river to be named an SSSI in Britain. At 134-miles long it the fifth longest river in the UK, and runs along the border of England from Plynlimon, the Cambrian Mountains' highest point, down to the Severn Estuary. It criss-crosses the English counties of Gloucestershire and Herefordshire along the way, before winding back into Wales to its mouth in the Monmouthshire town of Chepstow.

As well as being the Wye Valley's centrepiece, the river also serves as a good route to follow when exploring some of the AONB's many landmarks. There are launch points for canoeists and kayakers along the way, and the riverside can be followed on horseback, or by climbing the rocks of the limestone gorge.

The Wye Valley Walk is a 136-mile trek which takes around twelve days to complete. Broken down into eight more manageable walks, the longest starts at Chepstow Castle overlooking the Wye.

The woods which line the river's banks are of international importance, and can be seen on the first part of the walk from Chepstow to Monmouth, a 17-mile journey through sometimes dense forestry along the lower Wye gorge. The gorge's widest point is approximately 2 miles across at Welsh Bicknor, which, despite the name, is actually in England, just south of the village of Goodrich in Herefordshire. After reaching Monmouth, the Wye Valley Walk heads northwards with routes to Ross-on-Wye, Hereford, Hay-on-Wye, Builth Wells and Rhayader before ending at Plynlimon.

Stand-out landmarks are the Gothic splendour of Tintern Abbey, and Monmouth Castle, the birthplace of Henry V. A less obvious landmark, but one which offers panoramic views across the land, is Beacon Hill on Trellech Plateau near the village of Trellech. The heavily wooded area is full of wildlife, and if you keep your eyes and ears open as night falls in the summer you might hear the rare nocturnal nightjar bird.

Other rare species can be found at Croes Robert Wood nature reserve, an SSSI owned by Gwent Wildlife Trust. It is home to the endangered dormouse, along with rare trees, birds, butterflies and moths. For a glimpse back in time, Pentwyn Farm's flowers and hay meadows have remained as they would have looked hundreds of years ago, while its farm barn has been restored as accurately as possible.

Did You Know ...

When the Wye Valley inspired William Wordsworth to write 'Lines written a few miles above Tintern Abbey' in 1798, he claimed that the entire poem formed in his head while walking, before he even had time to sit down and put ink to paper.

2

WONDERS OF THE WORLD

When it comes to landmarks, they don't come much more spectacular than those selected by UNESCO, the United Nations Educational, Scientific and Cultural Organization.

In its mission statement, UNESCO says that it aims to help countries protect their 'natural and cultural heritage', and some of the more famous places from around the world which have been chosen for safe keeping include the Great Barrier Reef in Australia, the 'floating city' of Venice in Italy, the Grand Canyon in America, and the Taj Mahal in India.

In Wales, there are three UNESCO World Heritage Sites which stand shoulder to shoulder with some of the best in the world. They are Blaenavon Industrial Landscape, Pontcysyllte Aqueduct and Canal, and The Castles and Town Walls of King Edward in Gwynedd.

BLAENAVON INDUSTRIAL LANDSCAPE

The scarred industrial landscape surrounding the town of Blaenavon, which is spelled Blaenafon in Welsh, was declared a UNESCO World Heritage Site in 2000. Said to be the best of its kind in the UK, the area, which covers 13 square miles, records a period in Welsh history when the Industrial Revolution forever changed the face of the country and the lives of those living through such turbulent times.

By the nineteenth century, Blaenavon led the way in coal and iron production. Tightly knit communities sprang up around the

View of the National Coal Museum. © *Nessy-Pic (Wikimedia, CC BY-SA 3.0)*

works, and their way of life up to 1914 has now been preserved for future generations.

In 1984, Blaenavon's town centre was awarded conservation status, which means that much of it has retained the charm of earlier centuries, from the well-preserved terraced houses to its cobbled streets. It also produces a lot of it own food and drink, which can be sampled in a traditional setting.

A natural starting point when exploring Blaenavon is the Blaenavon World Heritage Centre. Housed in what was St Peter's church school, it was built in 1816 by Sarah Hopkins, the sister of ironworks' manager Samuel Hopkins, to provide free learning to the children of the workers. It continues in an educational capacity today, with a replica of a Victorian classroom.

Next to the centre is the workers' place of worship, St Peter's church, which was provided by the ironmasters in 1804. The Blaenavon Community Museum, in the former Workmen's Hall, was originally built in 1894 and contains the Cordell Museum, a tribute to author Alexander Cordell, who wrote extensively about life in industrial Wales, including his best-known work of fiction, *Rape of the Fair Country* (1959).

Blaenavon's most famous son, sportsman Ken Jones, is immortalised as a bronze statue by Paris-born sculptor Laury Dizengremel. The sprinter, and the first rugby union player to be inducted into the Welsh Sports Hall of Fame, scored the winning try against the All Blacks in 1953, and can be seen mid-run with ball in hand on Broad Street.

Outside of the town, the surrounding scenery can be viewed on board a steam train from the Blaenavon Heritage Railway, or on a boat along the Monmouthshire and Brecon Canal; cyclists can follow a bike route along the old mineral railway from Pontypool.

The area would once have been covered with the waste from the tips, and nature reserves like the Garn Lakes stand in stark contrast to days gone by. There are some fantastic panoramic views of the old industrial landscape available at the two main heritage sites, Big Pit National Coal Museum and Blaenavon Ironworks.

Coal production stopped at Big Pit National Coal Museum in 1980, but the pit has been maintained as a time capsule of the period, and offers guided tours of the old works. This involves donning a lamp-lit helmet and taking an authentic cage 100m underground into the darkness, just as the workers would have done on a daily basis.

Blaenavon Ironworks is home to what are said to be the best preserved furnaces from the eighteenth and nineteenth centuries. Of special note is the balance tower dating from 1839, which used water as a counterbalance to power a lift.

The miners' social history can also be explored in the cottages and the truck shop, an infamous store where the workers were paid in a currency only usable in the company's shop.

Did You Know ...

A brewery which used to serve up pints for the industrial workforce in Blaenavon is still going strong today. Rhymney Brewery was established in 1839, and back then beer wasn't just a tasty way to relax, but was actually safer to drink than water, which came with the risk of cholera.

PONTCYSYLLTE AQUEDUCT AND CANAL

Wales's most recent World Heritage Site was awarded protected status by UNESCO in 2009. Much like previous landmark Blaenavon, Pontcysyllte Aqueduct and Canal in the north-east of the country harks back to the Industrial Revolution, which changed the face of the country so dramatically.

Its story begins in 1795, when the Grade I listed landmark was conceived by Scottish civil engineer Thomas Telford. It was built under the supervision of English canal engineer William Jessop, and the unique demands of the location proved to be something of a headache for the architects. But they rose to the challenge, and their bold solution to the problem has since been described as a 'masterpiece'.

Tasked with finding a way for the Llangollen Canal to cross the River Dee, their plan took ten years to see fruition, and by the time it was completed in 1805 they had constructed nineteen cast iron pillars, whose arches spanned 307m, and stood 38m tall.

Pontcysyllte Aqueduct. © *Akke (Wikimedia, CC BY-SA 2.0)*

The canal linked the villages of Froncysyllte in the south to Trevor – spelled Trefor in Welsh – in the north, and the narrowboats began to sail along its waters during an opening ceremony on 26 November. The first to cross were six horse-drawn boats, two of which contained coal. With the canals continuing onwards towards Shropshire via the Chirk Aqueduct, this is said to mark the first time that an aqueduct connecting Wales with England had been used for commercial purposes.

Nowadays, Pontcysyllte Aqueduct and Canal is a tranquil spot to escape to, with the AONB area covering the entire length of the canal. It can be explored on foot with various structured paths leading through its 11 miles of scenery, while the National Trail's Offa's Dyke Path also takes in the aqueduct itself.

The ideal way to see the aqueduct would have to be on the water, and if you don't own your own narrowboat, there are motorised and traditional horse-drawn boat trips available. But if you have a fear of heights, don't look down – it only has railings on one side.

Other landmarks in the AONB include the water's starting point at Horseshoe Falls, just west of Llangollen. Also built by Telford, the artificial weir, which is a barrier used to alter the flow of the water, maintains the canal's height and is named after its distinctive shape.

The town of Llangollen is also home to the annual Llangollen International Eisteddfod, a cultural landmark that celebrates global music and dance. It takes place annually during the second week of July, and a highlight is the colourful Parade of Nations. From Llangollen, the Llangollen Steam Railway sets off into the Dee Valley.

Just outside Trevor is the Trevor Basin, a canal basin by the aqueduct which allows boats to turn and unload. Next to the village is Tŷ Mawr Country Park in Cefn Mawr. Set beneath the arches of Cefn Viaduct, it is an area where you might see salmon jumping from the water. Slightly further downstream is another of Telford's aqueducts at Chirk, home of the landmark Chirk Castle. Chirk Aqueduct was completed in 1801, and the viaduct, which was added nearly half a century later, connects Wales to England over the Ceiriog Valley.

THE CASTLES AND TOWN WALLS OF KING EDWARD IN GWYNEDD

In 1986, four of Wales's most well-preserved fortresses combined to form the country's first UNESCO World Heritage Site. The castles of Beaumaris and Harlech, along with the castles and fortifications which surround Conwy and Caernarfon, became collectively known as The Castles and Town Walls of King Edward in Gwynedd.

When Edward I invaded Wales in the thirteenth century, he set about defending the Kingdom of Gwynedd against rebellion. To achieve this, he turned to James of St George, the royal architect who has been dubbed 'the greatest military engineer of the time'.

The defences created during that period would play an important role in the history of Wales for centuries to come. They were the scene of many a clash during Owain Glyndŵr's uprising, as well as the Wars of the Roses in the fifteenth century, and by the nineteenth century the sublime beauty of the ruins was attracting the the likes of painter J.M.W. Turner for much more civilised reasons.

Now restored and in the care of Cadw, the Welsh government's historic environment service, ongoing restoration maintains them as tourist attractions, and buffer zones have been put in place to ensure that their views are protected.

Beaumaris Castle

Beaumaris Castle (Castell Biwmares) was Edward I's final castle to be built on Welsh soil. Standing in the town of Beaumaris, it is bordered by fields on the island of Anglesey, and looks, for all intents and purposes, like a finely constructed fortress. But it might surprise some to discover that it was actually left unfinished. With Edward's focus, and his funds, distracted by fighting the Scottish and the French, he left the castle incomplete.

Not that it was a small castle to finish. In fact, everyone living in the nearby village of Llanfaes had to be forcibly relocated 12 miles away to accommodate it. Constructed using stone from the local area, it also proved to be Edward's final moat-surrounded castle, and its main means of defense was its 'walls within walls' design. This meant that if anyone attacking the castle managed to penetrate the outer wall, they would be met with yet another stone barrier to fight through.

Beaumaris Castle's history includes being captured by the Welsh for two years during Owain Glyndŵr's rebellion, before falling into a state of ruin in the second half of the seventeenth century.

Conwy Castle and Town Walls

Conwy Castle (Castell Conwy) is considered by many to be the finest of Edward I's castles in Wales. Part of the 'wall town of Conwy' programme, it dominates the skyline as you approach the town, with its eight gigantic towers and two barbicans (fortified gateways) to greet would-be attackers on arrival. A vast rectangular fortress which was strategically built on a coastal ridge, what might have once served as the ideal look-out location for defenders, it now offers panoramic views across the estuary instead.

Inside the castle's walls is the great hall, which really does live up to its 'great' moniker, along with countless rooms, chambers and a royal chapel for worship. But unlike the invader's others castles, no 'wall within wall' defence was considered necessary here, thanks to Conwy Castle's naturally solid rock foundation.

In 1399, it hosted Richard II when he was in search of a place to lie low, and two years later it was held by the Welsh during Owain Glyndŵr's rebellion.

Caernarfon Castle and Town Walls

Caernarfon Castle (Castell Caernarfon) really is a monster of a castle. It is the very definition of an impenetrable fortress, and potential invaders must have felt defeated by just looking at it. Built on the site of an eleventh-century Norman motte-and-bailey castle (a fortification erected on an area of raised earth), Caernarfon was chosen for its strategic position looking down on the Afon Seiont river.

With its colour co-ordinated stones and polygonal towers, its most striking feature is the Eagle Tower, a ten-sided accommodation tower from which the Welsh flags now fly.

Caernarfon Castle. © *Manfred Heyde (Wikimedia CC BY-SA 2.5)*

Much like Beaumaris Castle, while it might look complete from the outside, there are parts inside which were never finished.

The castle also has a long history with the English Princes of Wales. In 1284, the first non-Welsh prince was born in the castle, and fast forward a few centuries and Prince Edward, who would later become Edward VIII, was invested there in 1911, followed by Charles, Prince of Wales, in 1958.

Another target for the men of Owain Glyndŵr during the uprising, by the nineteenth century Caernarfon Castle was left in a state of neglect.

Harlech Castle
Harlech Castle (Castell Harlech) was built with a purpose in mind: surveillance. And centuries later, that's exactly what we can use it for today. The castle's vantage point is the perfect place to survey the surrounds of Harlech, although we'd probably be looking out at the waters of Cardigan Bay and the peaks of Snowdonia rather than any approaching armies.

From a financial point of view, Harlech was one of the cheaper of Edward's castles, and was built from local stone in a location chosen for its proximity to the Irish Sea. This allowed it to be resupplied from the ocean along an ingenious stairway which still leads to the base of the cliff.

Once again utilising the concentric 'walls within walls' defence, it has an outer and an inner ring of towers, and an imposing main gatehouse. At the turn of the fifteenth century, it was briefly taken by Owain Glyndŵr, and was later captured by the House of Lancaster during the Wars of the Roses, who held on for seven years until the House of York forced them to relinquish it.

Did You Know ...

The lyrics to the popular Welsh song 'Men of Harlech', which can be heard booming around rugby stadiums and featured in the films *How Green Was My Valley* (1941) and *Zulu* (1964), are said to be based on the siege at the castle in 1468, during which a small group of vastly outnumbered men fought valiantly against an invading army.

3

THE SEVEN WONDERS OF WALES

The Seven Wonders of Wales (*Saith Rhyfeddod Cymru*) are a traditional list of seven 'must-see' places in north Wales.

They were compiled into a rhyme in the eighteenth or nineteenth century, and while the author is unknown, it is thought to have been the work of an Englishman who was visiting the area at the time. It goes like this:

Pistyll Rhaeadr and Wrexham steeple,
Snowdon's mountain without its people,
Overton yew trees, St Winefride's well,
Llangollen bridge and Gresford bells.

Remarkably, all seven can still be seen to this day, although not without alterations in some cases.

PISTYLL RHAEADR

At nearly 80m high Pistyll Rhaeadr, which translates as 'spring of the waterfall', has been described as the 'highest single-drop waterfall in Wales'. While this claim might not be accurate – the Devil's Appendix in Snowdonia has a single-drop waterfall of 93m – it still makes a fantastic landmark and a 'wonder of Wales'.

Just outside the village of Llanrhaeadr-ym-Mochnant in Powys, Pistyll Rhaeadr is formed by the Afon Disgynfa, and falls in three stages into the River Rhaeadr. The longest of these stages is about 40m. It is accessible to the public, and a visit can be combined with a walk around the Berwyn Mountains.

Pistyll Rhaeadr. © *Velela (Wikimedia, CC BY-SA 3.0)*

Did You Know ...

The Berwyn Mountains were the scene of one of Wales's most widely reported UFO sightings. In 1974, strange lights and sounds were reported in the sky, but they have since been dismissed as the combination of an earthquake and a meteor shower.

ST GILES'S CHURCH

Anyone heading to Wrexham can't fail but to notice the tower of St Giles's church, more than 40m high, which can be seen for miles around. And while it might be referred to as a steeple in the verse, it is very much a tower – which, admittedly, doesn't rhyme as well with the word 'people'. Now a Grade I listed building, the church dates from the fourteenth century and was given a huge facelift in the fifteenth. Work on the tower itself began in the sixteenth century.

Inside the church are sculptures of Lady Margaret Beaufort, who was King Henry VII's mother, and her third husband Thomas, Lord Stanley. They can be seen in the corbels, which are structural pieces of stone on the arches of the chancel. Other artistic treasures include a Doom painting depicting the Last Judgement, along with wooden medieval carvings.

Outside the church is the final resting place of Elihu Yale, the American of Welsh decent who lent his name to Yale University, with Yale being an Anglicisation of the Welsh name *Iâl*.

Did You Know ...

Reginald Heber's hymn 'From Greenland's Icy Mountains' was composed at St Giles's church, and received its first performance there in 1819.

OVERTON YEW TREES

In the Wrexham town of Overton-on-Dee, which is often shortened to Overton or Owrtyn in Welsh, can be found the twenty-one Overton yew trees referred to in the rhyme.

Planted between the third and twelfth centuries in the grounds of St Mary the Virgin church on High Street, the oldest tree is said to be at least 2,000 years old – older than the church itself, which can trace its origins back to the Norman period, and which still has nave pillars remaining from the time.

The eldest tree is distinctive as being the one which is supported by wooden posts, while the most recent addition was planted in 1992 by Queen Elizabeth II, who visited the town to mark its 700th anniversary.

ST WINEFRIDE'S WELL

Since the seventh century, pilgrims have flocked to St Winefride's Well and its miraculous spring. The 'Lourdes of Wales' is a Grade I listed holy well in Holywell, with the Flintshire town taking its name from the landmark.

According to the legend, it was the scene of a rather gruesome incident involving St Winifred (Santes Gwenffrewi). When Winifred spurned the advances of an unwanted suitor Caradoc, the son of a Welsh prince, he retaliated by cutting off her head. The holy well is said to stand at the scene of the decapitation, on the exact spot where her head landed. But there is something of a happy ending to the story. St Winifred's uncle St Beuno, who is claimed to have brought seven dead people back to life, revived her lifeless corpse.

In the fifteenth century, a chapel was built by Margaret Beaufort, Countess of Richmond and Derby, above the well. Some of the famous names who are said to have visited the well to ask for divine assistance over the centuries include Richard I ahead of his crusade, Henry V, Edward Oldcorne and others connected with the Gunpowder Plot of 1605, James II and his wife Mary of Modena, and a young Queen Victoria in 1828.

LLANGOLLEN BRIDGE

The Llangollen Bridge in Denbighshire was the first stone bridge to cross the River Dee. It is at least the third bridge to stand on the spot, and, having survived floods and rushing waters, is now a Grade I listed structure and a Scheduled Ancient Monument. Dating from the sixteenth century, it was widened in the nineteenth and twentieth centuries, and a stone tower was added in the 1860s, but this was demolished in the 1930s.

The first bridge to span the river was constructed around the twelfth century for packhorses to cross, with the second built by

John Trevor (Ieuan Trefor) during his time as Bishop of St Asaph in the middle of the fourteenth century.

GRESFORD BELLS

All Saints' church in the village of Gresford, Wrexham, is home to the thirteenth-century Gresford bells. The church, as we see it today, dates from the thirteenth century, with modifications made in the fourteenth and fifteenth centuries. It has a distinctive sandy brown colour thanks to the local stone used in its construction.

The Grade I listed building is considered to be dispropor-tionately large when compared to the area's population, which has led some people to speculate that it might once have played an important part in pilgrimages. The bells themselves are a 'wonder' due to the clarity of their tone. In 1877, the eight bells were adapted to allow them to be rung by a single person, and are still rung regularly for church services and on 5 November, an annual local tradition.

Much like Overton, the church can also lay claim to having some pretty impressive yew trees in the surrounding grounds.

SNOWDON

Not just a wonder of Wales, Snowdon is a wonder of the world. And the country's highest mountain is looked at in detail in the next chapter …

4

CLIMBING THE HIGHEST PEAKS

When Welsh historian Sir Owen M. Edwards wrote a history of Wales, simply entitled *Wales* (1901), he opened with the line 'Wales is a land of mountains'. And he isn't wrong.

Wales is more than blessed with its fair share of mountains and hills, and when it comes to landmarks, they form some of the country's most spectacular locations, including arguably its number one attraction.

But while Snowdonia, and its highest peak Snowdon, might get all the plaudits as a world-renowned destination, there's no shortage of other high points to explore across the land. There's the Cribarth hill in the Brecon Beacons National Park, for example, which is known as the Sleeping Giant because – from the right angle – it really does look like a slumbering giant lying flat on his back. And then there's Sugar Loaf, a prominence just outside Llanwrtyd Wells which offers some incredible views across Carmarthenshire, and even has its own railway stop on the scenic Heart of Wales line.

From the Cambrian Mountains in the middle of the country, to the Black Mountains in the south, these summits formed in the Ice Age have served as protector in times of war, a source of leisure in times of peace, and as a constant inspiration for centuries of travellers.

THE WELSH 3000s

The Welsh 3000s is the collective name given to fifteen mountains in Wales which are 3,000ft (914m) or higher. It also lends its name to the Welsh 3000s Challenge, where adventurers can attempt to walk all fifteen in a twenty-four-hour period, which is made slightly easier by the fact that they can all be found in adjoining mountain ranges. About 26 miles in length, a newer addition following its reclassification is Glyder Fach's Castell y Gwynt, making it potentially a sixteen-peak challenge, while Carnedd Gwenllian is sometimes skipped over for not being a summit in and of itself.

The mountains are:

Snowdon
Snowdon: 1,085m
Garnedd Ugain: 1,065m
Crib Goch: 923m

Glyderau
Elidir Fawr: 924m
Y Garn: 947m
Glyder Fawr: 1,001m
Castell y Gwynt: 972m
Glyder Fach: 994m
Tryfan: 918m

Carneddau
Pen yr Ole Wen: 978m
Carnedd Dafydd: 1,044m
Carnedd Llewelyn: 1,064m
Yr Elen: 962m
Foel Grach: 976m
Carnedd Gwenllian: 926m
Foel-fras: 942m

SNOWDONIA

When it comes to Welsh landmarks, they don't come much more awe-inspiring than Wales's highest mountain ranges.

With breathtaking views which could give the Alps a run for their money, Snowdonia in the north-west of the country is

View to Snowdon from Yr Aran. © *James@hopgrove (Wikimedia, CC BY-SA 3.0)*

where Sir Edmund Hillary, the New Zealand mountaineer who became the first man to climb Mount Everest, chose to train ahead of his expedition to conquer the world's biggest mountain.

Nowadays, it's much easier to reach the summits by walking along the 1,479 miles of public footpaths, or you could take the more luxurious route on board the Snowdon Mountain Railway.

In 1951, Snowdonia became the first of Wales's three national parks, and only the third in the United Kingdom behind the Peak District and the Lake District. It covers 823 square miles, and according to the 2011 census more than 26,000 people live within its boundaries, of whom nearly 60 per cent can speak the Welsh language.

The vast area, which lies partly in Gwynedd and partly in Conwy, is named after Snowdon, its highest peak. The meaning of Snowdonia's Welsh name, Eryri, has been the source of much speculation. It was thought to be a reference to the Welsh word for eagle, *eryr*, possibly making it 'the Land of the Eagles'. But a more recent explanation suggest that it derives from the Latin word for Highlands, *oriri*.

Not that it's all about the mountains. Snowdonia has 37 miles of coastline, and is a designated SAC with some unique plants, birds and animals, some of which have been named after the area. These include the Snowdonia hawkweed, a bright yellow plant which was believed to have been extinct since the 1950s, until it was rediscovered in Cwm Idwal in 2002; the Snowdon Lily, a flowering Arctic-alpine plant; and the multi-coloured Snowdon beetle. While not unique, rare animals include otters, polecats, and the feral goats which are thought to have called the peaks their home for around 10,000 years.

The Mountain Ranges
The mountain ranges of Snowdonia can be split up into four sections, with the northern peaks being the most popular with visitors. This is where you'll find the country's highest mountains, including Snowdon itself, a part of the Snowdon Massif range which has an elevation of 1,085m. Other mountain groups in the north include the Glyderau, home of the distinctive fin-shaped Tryfan mountain in the Ogwen Valley; Carneddau, which has the largest area of ground more than 900m high in Wales and England; Moel Hebog, which looms over the village of Beddgelert; and the smaller Nantlle Ridge, which is favoured by walkers because it offers great views but is less of a challenge.

In the centre of the mountain ranges are the Moelwynion. The highest peak here is Moel Siabod, and if the weather is fine, from the top of its 872m you can see thirteen of Wales's fourteen highest peaks without even turning your head.

The third region is the least busy, which makes it a good choice for those looking to avoid the crowds. There you'll find the Rhinogydd range near Harlech, which has a high point of 756m at Y Llethr. The region is named after two of its more well-known peaks, the rocky Rhinog Fawr and Rhinog Fach, and has a vast moorland area called Migneint, which, along with the two Arenig mountains, Arenig Fawr and Arenig Fach, and Dduallt, form the Migneint-Arenig-Dduallt SAC.

Finally, the southerly cairn-filled region contains arguably Snowdonia's second-most famous mountain, Cadair Idris. Towering over Dolgellau at 893m, its name in English – which is now thought to be a mistranslation – is Idris's Chair. The Idris in question is thought to be either a legendary giant, or possibly the seventh-century prince Idris ap Gwyddno, who was known as Idris Gawr, Idris the Giant. Its three peaks are Penygader, which is the mountain's summit and the 'head of the chair'; the second-highest summit, the rocky Mynydd Moel, or the 'bare mountain'; and Cyfrwy, the 'saddle', which overlooks Llyn y Gadair, a relatively shallow lake famed for being a hotspot for Welsh fairy folk the Tylwyth Teg. Also in the south is the Aran Fawddwy mountain in the Aran range, which at 905m high makes it the highest in Wales south of Snowdon.

The Mountains as a Muse

Snowdonia has been a source of inspiration for the artistically inclined for centuries, with the likes of local landscape specialist Sir Kyffin Williams, and arguably Britain's most celebrated painter J.M.W. Turner, capturing its lofty peaks on canvas.

The Arenig Fawr mountain is referenced in English poet Sir Edmund Spenser's epic poem *The Faerie Queene* (1590), in which a young King Arthur's foster-father Old Timon is said to live 'Under the foot of Rauran mossy hore'. Rauran is said to

Castell y Gwynt on Glyder Fach. © *Llywelyn2000 (Wikimedia, CC BY-SA 4.0)*

be Arenig, while his home would have stood on the spot of the Roman fort Caer Gai.

In the early twentieth century celebrated Welsh artist Augustus John, who is perhaps more famous for his portraits, along with fellow Welshman James Dickson Innes and Australian Derwent Lees, became known collectively as the Arenig school of painters, where they scoured the valley in search of the perfect painting locations.

In more recent times, Disney headed to the epic Glyder Fach mountain in 1981 to shoot scenes for the fantasy film *Dragonslayer*. It has a dramatic rocky outcrop on its summit called Castell y Gwynt (Castle of the Winds) which has an elevation of 972m. Nearby is the Cantilever Stone, or Y Gwyliwr, a giant rock which hangs in the air and looks like it might topple at any moment, but is just a trick of the perspective.

The Legends
Adding a magical twist to the landmarks are the ancient myths and legends which surround them.

There are several locations that feature in the text of *The Mabinogion*, a collection of ancient Welsh tales which includes early references to King Arthur. Arthur himself is said to have slain the giant Rhitta Gawr on Snowdon, who held court on what is now his final resting place. The king's name can be found in Ffynnon Cegin Arthur (Well of Arthur's Kitchen), a natural spring which is enclosed in a brick chamber, and his magical sword Excalibur is said to be submerged in the waters of Llyn Llydaw, Llyn Dinas and Llyn Ogwen – a claim which is also made by several other rivers across Wales.

Snowdonia could also be the birthplace of Y Ddraig Goch, the red dragon found on the Welsh flag. In the fifth century, the warlord Vortigern is said to have attempted to build a fortress in Dinas Emrys near Beddgelert, but every morning when the workers awoke they would find their hard work from the previous day demolished. A young boy named Myrddin Emrys – who would become known as the wizard Merlin in Arthurian mythology – explained that it was caused by a red dragon and a white dragon who were fighting underground. This tale was later developed into an analogy for the native Britons fighting the invading Saxons, a battle which the Britons (the red dragon) would eventually win.

One of the more beautiful places to visit is also home to one of Wales's more tragic legends. The village of Beddgelert takes its name from the Welsh words *bedd* and *Gelert*, which means 'Gelert's grave'. In the folk tale, Gelert was a faithful hound who saved his master's baby from an attacking wolf, but was mistakenly slain when Prince Llewelyn the Great returned home to find the child disturbed and the dog covered in blood. A mound created in the eighteenth century is said to be Gelert's final resting place, and a sculpture, along with many other dog-related curiosities, can be found in the hamlet.

The Snowdon Summit Visitor Centre and Mountain Railway
At the top of Wales's highest mountain you'll find Hafod Eryri, the Snowdon Summit Visitor Centre. Opened in 2009, it was designed by Ray Hole, and won the National Eisteddfod of Wales Gold Medal for Architecture in the same year. It offers panoramic views of the world below. A building is known to have stood on the same spot since at least the 1820s, replaced in 1930 by a new building designed by Sir Clough Williams-Ellis of Portmeirion fame.

The easiest way to reach Hafod Eryri is to hop on one of Snowdon Mountain Railway's trains in Llanberis, which have been shepherding visitors up the mountainside since 1896. Inspired by a visit to the Swiss Alps, four of the original made-in-Switzerland trains are still in use today.

Another nearby railway landmark, and another way to see some of the surrounding area's landmarks, is Ffestiniog Railway. The narrow-gauge railway has steam trains which are now more than 150 years old, and is owned by what is said to be the 'oldest surviving railway company in the world', the Festiniog Railway Company, which is spelled with a single F retained from the nineteenth century. Setting off from the harbour in Porthmadog to the slate-mining town of Blaenau Ffestiniog, the company also runs the Welsh Highland Railway, a 25-mile journey which starts in Caernarfon and heads back to Porthmadog.

Did You Know …

Snowdonia is one of the wettest spots in the UK, and the wettest spot in Snowdonia is the Crib Goch (Red Ridge), which has an average of 4,473mm of rain a year.

THE BLACK MOUNTAINS

The heather-covered Black Mountains (Y Mynyddoedd Duon) on the eastern end of the Brecon Beacons National Park offer spectacular views across south-east Wales and England.

Forming a rough triangle on the map, they start in Abergavenny in the east, head west to the village of Llangorse, and up north towards Hay-on-Wye. A favourite with ramblers, mountain bikers and horse riders, as well as those who like to get airbound on gliders, the area is covered predominantly by old red sandstone mountains.

Looking north along the Pen Twyn Mawr ridge. © *James Ayres (Wikimedia, CC BY-SA 2.0)*

Sprawling across the counties of Powys and Monmouthshire, the mountains also spill over the English border into Herefordshire. The 677m-tall Hay Bluff mastiff stands on the border of both countries, while Offa's Dyke Path, one of Britain's National Trails, follows the border over the Black Mountains en route from Prestatyn in the north to the Severn Estuary in the south.

The Black Mountains have three Marilyns taller than 600m, the highest being Waun Fach with an elevation of 811m. Its summits include Rhos Dirion, 713m high, and Twmpa, or Lord Hereford's Knob, at 690m.

The trio is rounded off with Twyn Llech (Black Mountain) which stands 703m high on the border with England, and Mynydd Troed, which is 609m high, and is said to resemble a foot when seen from the 719m Pen Allt-Mawr ridge.

A popular Marilyn with walkers is Sugar Loaf in Monmouthshire. Named after its resemblance to a sugar loaf, at 596m high it offers views as far as Shropshire and Somerset. Just outside Abergavenny, its wooded area is an SSSI, and is home to Welsh mountain sheep. It even has its own vineyard in Dummar Farm.

When it comes to historical landmarks, the distinctive Ysgyryd Fawr (Skirrid) in Monmouthshire is the site of an Iron Age hill fort, as well as the ruins of a medieval chapel. At 486m tall, the easterly mountain's Welsh name translates as 'the great shattered hill', and the place of pilgrimage is said to have 'shattered' at the moment Jesus Christ was crucified. It is also the home of the Devil's Table, a plinth where the evil one is claimed to have played cards with a giant. The mountain's English name is more well known in popular culture thanks to the infamous Skirrid Mountain Inn, which is claimed to be both the oldest and the most haunted pub in Wales.

From picturesque churches to idyllic farmyards, there are countless places of interest in and around the range. For wildlife, there's Coed-y-Cerrig National Nature Reserve at the foot of the mountains in Abergavenny. Its name means Wood of Stones, and it packs a lot of trees, insects, animals and plants into a small space.

Hay-on-Wye, the 'Welsh town of books' at the northern point, is a magnet for bibliophiles with around thirty bookshops.

World famous for the annual Hay Festival, the literature and arts festival draws around 25,000 people to the village each year – a tight squeeze for a hamlet with a population of around 1,500.

On the eastern edge of the Black Mountains is the village of Llanvihangel Crucorney, the birthplace of one of Wales's most famous men of words, Raymond Williams. His final works of fiction, *People of the Black Mountains, Volume 1:The Beginning* (1989) and *Volume 2: The Eggs of the Eagle* (1990), are set in the area.

Did You Know …

The Black Mountains are often confused with the Black Mountain, which is a range on the opposite end of Brecon Beacons National Park. The Black Mountain range crosses the counties of Carmarthenshire and Powys on the western side of the park, with Fan Brycheiniog being its highest peak at 802m.

THE CAMBRIAN MOUNTAINS

The Cambrian Mountains (Mynyddoedd Cambria) are a vast, tranquil area of gorges, moorland and valleys, untarnished and undisturbed by modern-day motor vehicles. In fact, there is only one single main route crossing the entire range, which makes plotting a course nice and easy.

Historically, the name Cambrian Mountains referred to most of the mountains in Wales, including fellow landmark ranges Snowdonia and the Black Mountains. But it now refers to a series of ranges predominantly in mid-Wales, stretching from Plynlimon in north Ceredigion into Powys and down towards Mynydd Mallaen at the top of Carmarthenshire.

The area is described as the 'watershed' of Wales, due to the fact that ten rivers – the Severn, Wye, Elan, Irfon, Tywi, Cothi, Teifi, Ystwyth, Rheidol and Twymyn – all start there. One of the tallest waterfalls in Wales is Pistyll y Llyn in the Cambrian Mountains, which falls for around 160m in two main drops, the longest of which is 91m.

In contrast, the range is also home to the 'desert of Wales', but not because of any sand. The Elenydd and surrounding area that crosses the counties of Ceredigion and Powys were romantically dubbed the 'Green Desert of Wales' by nineteenth-century travel writers who came across its wild, largely unpopulated, and inaccessible blanket bog.

The highest point in the Cambrian Mountains is Plynlimon, the Welsh name for which, Pumlumon, translates as 'the big five-peaked mountain'. It offers views to its fellow landmark ranges in the Brecon Beacons in the south and Snowdonia in the north, with its tallest peak being Pen Pumlumon Fawr at 752m.

The massif was once an area of industrial importance, and remains of old works, from chimneys to waterwheels, can still be seen across the land. The Silver Mountain Experience, a former silver-lead mine, is now open to the public. Other landmarks include the Stag, a mining debris patch which is said to resemble the antlered animal when seen from Cwm Rheidol Reservoir, and the abandoned Cwmystwyth metal mines, a designated

View towards Pumlumon Arwystli from Carn Hyddgen. © *Nigel Brown (Wikimedia, CC BY-SA 2.0)*

Scheduled Ancient Monument, which were mined from the Bronze Age to more recent times.

The second-highest mountain in the range is the 741m Pen Pumlumon Arwystli, the source of the River Severn, while the River Wye begins just below the third-highest mountain, the 727m Pen Pumlumon Llygad-bychan.

A good vantage point is from Foel Fadian hill which, while not as tall as the surrounding mountains, offers views of the peaks of Plynlimon, the many cliffs and waterfalls, and the Glaslyn nature reserve's upland lake. Its summit Dewey is 564m high.

Archaeological finds in the area include barrows and mounds, with a pair of Bronze Age cairns named Crugiau Merched (Ladies' Cairns) on the 462m peak of Carmarthenshire's Mynydd Mallaen, and ancient standing stones Maen Bach nearby. Gold mining began in the area in the Roman period, and the National Trust's Dolaucothi Gold Mines is open to visitors.

Off the beaten track in a more secluded spot outside Llanddewi Brefi is Soar y Mynydd chapel. The Welsh Calvinist Methodist chapel, which was built in 1822 for those working on the distant hills, is said to be Wales's 'most remote' and 'most isolated' chapel. Still a pilgrimage destination today, it can be reached by travelling along the time-honoured roads from Tregaron.

The Cambrian Mountains are a popular destination for trout fishers, while birdwatchers can spot the reintroduced red kites and other birds of prey who call the mountains home, such as the hen harrier, peregrine falcon and merlin.

One way to go in search of these landmarks is on board one of the Vale of Rheidol Railway's steam trains, which travel nearly 12 miles between Aberystwyth to Devil's Bridge, with open carriages in the summer to take in all of the scenery.

Did You Know …

Unlike Snowdonia and the Brecon Beacons, the Cambrian Mountains are not a National Park. A proposal was submitted in the 1960s, but it was opposed by the authorities and farmers from the local area.

PEN Y FAN

With an elevation of 886m, Pen y Fan in the Brecon Beacons National Park is south Wales's highest peak. And right next to it is Corn Du which, standing at 873m, is south Wales's second-highest peak.

At the top of the old red sandstone mountain is a Bronze Age cairn marked with a National Trust plaque on its stone cist. On a clear day landmarks from across Wales can be seen from this vantage point that takes in both the Black and Cambrian Mountains, stretching as far north-east as Shropshire in England. Along with Cribyn at 795m, and Y Gyrn at 619m, the summits are a popular destination for walkers and runners, as well as for the UK's military, who use the mountain for exercise purposes.

One landmark which was born in tragic circumstances is Tommy Jones's Obelisk, erected in memory of a 5-year-old boy who lost his way and died of exhaustion and exposure in 1900. The inscription on the granite pillar on the approach to Corn Du reads:

> This obelisk marks the spot where the body of Tommy Jones aged 5 was found. He lost his way between Cwm Llwch Farm and the Login on the night of August 4th 1900. After an anxious search of 29 days his body was found on September 2nd.

Pen-y-Fan summit from the ridge. © *AndyScott (Wikimedia, CC BY-SA 4.0)*

5

GETTING BACK TO NATURE

When Tom Jones sang about the green, green grass of home, the number one hit might have been written by an American from Nashville, but it still perfectly captured the natural beauty of his native land.

Wales is very much a green country, with large amounts of protected forestry to be explored. It is also a land, for better or for worse, which is blessed with more than its fair share of rainfall, which has created some of the awe-inspiring lakes and rivers which flow through the countryside.

From the acres of ancient woodland to gigantic waterfalls, this chapter takes a look at some of nature's incredible Welsh landmarks.

THE NATIONAL BIRD OF WALES

The red kite is considered to be, unofficially at least, the national bird of Wales. But it wasn't that long ago that these birds of prey with their distinctive V-shaped tails were pushed to near extinction, and it is only thanks to some incredibly hard work that their numbers have been bolstered in the country.

There are now thought to be around 1,000 breeding pairs in Wales, and they are particularly plentiful in the counties of Powys and Carmarthenshire and in Ceredigion, which is home to one of the best places to see them in the wild.

The valley of Bwlch Nant yr Arian, a Forestry Commission in the village of Ponterwyd outside of Aberystwyth, became a red kite feeding station in 1999. It is a huge success, and it is

Red Kite *Milvus milvus*, Bwlch Nant yr Arian, Ceredigion. © *Hannah Gilbert (Wikimedia, CC BY 2.0)*

possible to see more than 150 birds descending at feeding time, which takes place daily by the lake. Vantage points to watch from include a nearby bird hide, or from the centre's cafe. While there, you can take in the views over the Cambrian Mountains and Cardigan Bay, and follow a waymarked trail on foot, bike or horseback, one of which leads towards the feeding frenzy.

For an even greater number of red kites, as many as 600 are said to flock to the Red Kite Feeding Centre on Gigrin Farm, a working farm near the market town of Rhayader in Powys; they are fed by the farmer, and are joined by buzzards and corvids. The feeding can be seen from bird hides just a few metres from the action.

Meanwhile, those exploring the Brecon Beacons can head for the Llanddeusant Red Kite Feeding Station in Carmarthenshire's Black Mountain range. The birds are fed regularly, and around fifty red kites, along with buzzards and ravens, can be observed from the village of Llanddeusant.

Did You Know …

A rare white kite has been seen at Bwlch Nant yr Arian, which is actually a leucistic red kite, a genetic condition which results in loss of colour pigmentation.

RIVERS AND LAKES

River Dee
The River Dee (Afon Dyfrdwy) is a river which forms part of the border between Wales and England. Nearly 70 miles long, from its source in the Dduallt mountain in Snowdonia it winds past several Welsh landmarks, crossing over into Chester on its way to the sea. Three of its largest watery landmarks are Bala Lake, Llyn Brenig and Llyn Celyn.

Bala Lake
Bala Lake (Llyn Tegid) in Gwynedd is Wales's largest lake. More than 40m deep, it was also Wales's largest natural body of water until its level was raised by Scottish civil engineer Thomas Telford to assist the planned Ellesmere Canal between Wales and England. Its 1.87 square miles of seemingly bottomless, crystal clear waters were formed in the Ice Age by a blocked glacial valley. Now a part of Snowdonia National Park, it is nearly 4 miles in length and half a mile in width.

Adding to the lake's appeal are the mysteries surrounding its name and origin. According to the legendary Welsh bard Taliesin, the husband of the enchantress Ceridwen was named Tegid Foel, which means Bald Tegid, and his submerged court can be glimpsed under the waters by moonlight. As far back as the twelfth century, Gerald of Wales refers to it as Penmelesmere,

Bala Lake. © *Necrothesp (Wikimedia, CC BY-SA 3.0)*

and the colourful English travel writer George Borrow wrote in his travelogue *Wild Wales* (1856) that the name meant 'Lake of Beauty'.

A lake of beauty it might be, but it is also home to Wales's nearest equivalent to the Scottish water serpent the Loch Ness Monster. Dubbed Tessie, a mythological afanc has been sighted in its waters for centuries, with monster hunters and TV crews spending days on its banks in search of the camera-shy creature.

For swimmers, it is the final leg of the Loch, Lake, Llyn or Three-Lakes Challenge. A watery alternative to the National Three Peaks Challenge, it involves a five-person relay team swimming the combined 40 miles of Scotland, England and Wales's longest rivers. It starts with Scotland's Loch Awe, before heading to Windermere in England, and wrapping things up in Gwynedd.

Llyn Brenig
Llyn Brenig is a reservoir in the Denbigh Moors (Mynydd Hiraethog). The fourth-largest lake in Wales, it stands 366m high in the moorland area which borders the counties of Conwy and Denbighshire. Constructed and filled in the 1970s to manage the River Dee's flow, it covers 920 acres of land, and is 9 miles in length.

The area is rich in archaeological discoveries, with items from the Bronze Age discovered during its creation. Barrows and ring cairns can be seen in the surrounding area, while artefacts are on display in the visitors' centre.

Llyn Celyn

Llyn Celyn is, sadly, a landmark for all of the wrong reasons, and its symbolism is far more powerful than any connotations of beauty which might surround it nowadays. The 43m deep reservoir was created in the 1960s to supply water to Liverpool. In doing so, the Liverpool Corporation flooded Capel Celyn, a populated Welsh village rich in the native tongue and culture.

Despite being met by almost universal resistance in Wales, the proposal was rubber-stamped by parliament. There were protests and marches in the streets, and the official opening ceremony was cut short when protesters drowned out the speeches by chanting and severing the microphone wires.

On the fortieth anniversary of its creation in 2005, Liverpool City Council issued a statement apologising for their predecessors' actions: 'For any insensitivity by our predecessor Council at that time, we apologise and hope that the historic and sound relationship between Liverpool and Wales can be completely restored.'

Did You Know ...

While most places in Wales have, by now, settled on a common Welsh or English name, Afon Dyfrdwy, or the River Dee, is one of the few to change its name depending on where it is along the route.

Cregennan Lakes

Cregennan Lakes (Llynnau Cregennan) in the Snowdonia National Park are a pair of shimmering lakes beneath the slopes of landmark mountain Cadair Idris. They also have a fascinating story behind their potentially gruesome name.

Centuries ago, the Welsh chieftain Ednowain ap Bradwen was said to try lawbreakers at his nearby residence of Llys Bradwen, the site of which can be visited in the community of Arthog. If found guilty they would be hanged by the lake, and the name Cregennen is thought to be a mutation of the Welsh words *crog* and *gangen*, which translates as 'hanging branch (or bar)'. No such scenes disturb the beauty of the spot nowadays, which overlooks Afon Mawddach (Mawddach Estuary) from nearly 240m above sea level.

The lakes are more likely to attract fishermen than legendary lords now, looking to catch the wild brown trout to be found in both the small and the large lakes. For wildlife lovers, the sunnier weather brings with it the often well-hidden wheatears birds.

The larger of the two lakes is also home to a mythological island. According to legend, in ancient times the Celts would hurl their riches in to the 27-acre lake for good luck.

The Elan Valley Dams

The Elan Valley in Powys is a 70 square mile river valley with giant reservoirs, its own village, and its most popular attractions – its dams.

Work began on excavating the foundations for its six dams by the Birmingham Corporation in the late nineteenth

The Elan Valley Reservoirs. © *Amanda Slater (Wikimedia, CC BY-SA 2.0)*

century. Its most famous dam, Craig Goch, is in the Elan river, along with Pen-y-garreg, Garreg Ddu and Caban Coch. The Claerwen river is home to the Claerwen dam, and the unfinished Dol-y-Mynach.

The first to be built was the lowest of the six, Caban Coch. Craig Goch, which is also known as the Top Dam, followed soon after. The highest of the dams, it towers over the valley 317m above sea level. A fully functional Victorian masonry dam made from stone and brick, it has distinctive arches, along with a rather precarious-looking roadway along the top which overlooks the flowing waters below.

The Claerwen Dam is the most recent addition, having been opened by Queen Elizabeth II in October 1952. While all of the dams can be visited, Dol-y-Mynach is not accessible to motor vehicles, while Garreg Ddu is entirely submerged under the water.

Did You Know ...

The nearby Elan Village is the work of Barmouth-born Arts and Crafts architect Herbert Tudor Buckland. His only model village in his native land was designed for the workers and their families of the new dams.

Llangorse Lake
South Wales's largest lake can be found in the village of Llangorse, which falls within the boundaries of the Brecon Beacons National Park.

Llangorse Lake is the only place in Wales where you can see a crannog, an artificial island dwelling created in the water. Around 40m out from the shore, it is thought to date from the eighth or ninth century. Its walkway was created with oak planks, at the end of which is a stone, soil and brushwood platform.

The glacial lake is a mile long and can reach 7.5m in depth. An SSSI, the popular fishing spot can lay claim to being the place where the largest pike in the world was caught – well, kind of. Sadly, the boast that an angler hooked a 68lb pike on one occasion is unsubstantiated.

Giant pikes aside, anyone fishing the lake might want to keep an eye out for Gorsey, the nickname given to the creature said to lurk in its depths. The afanc, much like Tessie in Bala Lake, is said to eat anyone who takes a dip in its waters, and its appearance varies from a crocodile to a demon. It has been suggested that the afanc might in fact be a group of beavers, or possibly another super-sized pike.

Llyn y Fan Fach

Llyn y Fan Fach, which means Lake of the Small Hill, has the double distinction of not only being one of Wales's most awe-inspiring lakes, but also the home of one of its most well-known legends. Falling within the western boundaries of the Brecon Beacons National Park in Carmarthenshire's Black Mountain, it sits in a valley which was excavated by a glacier during the Ice Age.

With a depth of 29m, the dammed lake is a little off the beaten track, and the easiest way to see it is by looking down from one of the peaks on the Carmarthen Fans, with Picws Du and Waun Lefrith being favoured vantage points.

In the thirteenth century legend of the Lady of the Lake, a fair maiden rises from the water to be met by a young farmer from nearby Blaen Sawdde. She tells him that if he agrees to marry her he'll achieve great success and, dazzled by her beauty, he readily accepts. But there were two conditions – he must not hit her three times, or reveal her magical origins. This seemed like an easy enough set of requests, but over time he did indeed strike his wife lightly on three occasions. The Lady of the Lake, and her famous white cattle – the descendants of which can now be seen grazing at the National Trust's Dinefwr Park in Llandeilo – returned to their watery abode. Their offspring would grow up to become to renowned Physicians of Myddfai.

Legends aside, there is also plenty of wildlife to keep an eye out for. Birds of prey in the area include the buzzard, kestrel, and Wales's national bird, the red kite.

An even bigger watery landmark can be seen about 2 miles away from Llyn y Fan Fach, the appropriately named Llyn y Fan Fawr, with *fawr* being the Welsh word for 'big'.

WATERFALLS

Swallow Falls

Swallow Falls is the more romantic name given to the Rhaeadr Ewynnol waterfall system by tourists who, it is assumed, mispronounced the Welsh name which simply means 'foaming waterfall'.

The waters of the Afon Llugwy river flow from the River Conwy near Betws-y-Coed in Conwy, and create a series of waterfalls which crash over the dark rocks. Situated in the Snowdonia National Park, they can be seen from several places, with the most impressive views seen from the northern bank. The falls are at their most spectacular outside of the summer months, when the water is more visible through the foliage, and heavy rainfall adds to the dramatic effect.

Cenarth Falls

Cenarth Falls, in the Ceredigion village of Cenarth, is the site of an impressive series of waterfalls, jumping salmon, and the ancient secrets of navigating the waters in a coracle.

A coracle is a small, round, paddle-powered boat made of wicker or ash, a type of craft which has been used by fishermen for centuries. While not unique to Wales, coracles derive their name from the Welsh word *cwrwgl*, and have become a symbol of the country's heritage, being one of the few places in the world where they are still in use – albeit mainly for tourists.

The coracle museum at the National Coracle Centre, which has its own out-of-use seventeenth-century watermill, overlooks the series of falls in the River Teifi. Inside the museum, the coracle tradition is celebrated not only in Wales, but from as far afield as Iraq and Tibet.

The falls are well known for their salmon, which migrate up the river and can be seen leaping in the autumn.

Did You Know ...

If you want to see fish leaping in a more secluded spot, you can head for Henllan Falls just upstream.

Pwll-y-Wrach Waterfall

Pwll-y-Wrach waterfall, one of several Welsh locations to be named 'pool of the witch', can be found near the town of Talgarth in Powys. Running through it is the River Enig, and at its eastern end it diverges into two streams which plummet over the Bishop's Frome limestone rocks into a dark and eerie pool below – the witch's pool.

Enchanted water features aside, Pwll-y-Wrach Nature Reserve is an SSSI, which covers 17.5 hectares of woodland in the Brecon Beacons National Park. The reserve has seasonal flowers, and a range of wildlife.

Did You Know …

It is said that some of the Welsh places, such as at this nature reserve, which are named Pwll-y-Wrach, or Pwll y Wrach, were given their names because those accused of witchcraft were 'dunked' there.

Waterfall Country

Where do you start with an area known as Waterfall Country?

The waterfall-infested countryside at the head of the Vale of Neath really does live up to its moniker, and best of all, a large number of the waterfalls are easily accessible to the public. Crossing over into the Brecon Beacons National Park, Waterfall Country contains several SSSIs and SACs, and with so many falls to choose from, here are a few highlights.

Sgwd yr Eira: A landmark among landmarks, the breathtaking Sgwd yr Eira, which means Falls of Snow, on the Afon Hepste, is the best way to get up close and personal with a force of nature. You can walk behind the free-flowing waters and feel the spray on your face.

Sgwd Henrhyd: For a touch of Hollywood glamour, head to the Nant Llech river's Henrhyd Falls waterfall. It featured as the entrance to the Caped Crusader's batcave in *The Dark Knight Rises* (2012), starring Christian Bale as Batman; he, incidentally, was born not too far away in Haverfordwest. With a massive

A couple separated by a wall of water. © *Charlie Marshall (Wikimedia, CC BY 2.0)*

27m drop, it is the highest waterfall in the Brecon Beacons National Park.

Afon Mellte: The Mellte river has three stand-out waterfalls along its route, which are made extra special due to their close proximity to each other: Sgwd Clun-gwyn at the top, Sgwd Isaf Clun-gwyn in the middle, and Sgwd y Pannwr at the bottom.

Sgwd Gwladus: There's nothing like a good legend to add a little magic to a landmark, and the 'Lady's Falls' are so named after the daughter of the fifth-century prince Brychan of Brycheiniog. According to the tale, Gwladus fell in love with Einion, but her love went unrequited. As a result, her spirit is now said to flow in the waters which bear her name. Nearby is Sgwd Einion Gam, which is named after her loved one, but there is no easy route available, and it requires some tricky water crossing to reach it.

Aberdulais Falls: The waterfall at Aberdulais Falls is the centrepiece of the National Trust's wonderful tin works, which has lovingly preserved an important moment of Welsh industrial heritage. From the Dulais Valley it flows into a waterwheel 8.2m in diameter, which would have powered the rollers in the Victorian tinplate work.

Melincourt Falls: Melin Court Brook is home to a 24m waterfall, and is one of the landmarks captured by celebrated artist J.M.W. Turner during his tour of the Waterfall Country. Just outside the village of Resolven, it is part of a nature reserve area cared for by Wildlife Trust of South and West Wales.

Sychryd Cascade: The waters of the Afon Sychryd run between the rocks of Craig-y-Ddinas and Bwa Maen into a series of falls which flow over the rocky and eroded surface. There are also smaller falls around and above the Sychryd Cascade to be explored.

NATURE RESERVES AND FORESTS

The Lily Ponds at Stackpole Estate

From farmland to woodland, and beaches to cliffs, the National Trust's Stackpole Estate in the Pembrokeshire Coast National Park is 4.6 square miles of non-stop natural beauty.

The Lily Ponds, or Bosherston Lakes, is the collective name given to its *c.* 100 acres of lakes created in the eighteenth and nineteenth centuries by the earls of Cawdor, the estate's then owners. They can be crossed on the Grade II* listed Eight Arch Bridge, a major landmark which dates from 1797.

The estate is home to some immaculate beaches, including the secluded Barafundle, which can be accessed via Stackpole Quay harbour, and the dune-backed Broadhaven South at the end of the Bosherston Lakes.

The Stackpole Court mansion once stood at the heart of the estate, but it was torn down in the 1960s and only some of the outbuildings remain.

Did You Know ...

Welsh band Gorky's Zygotic Mynci named their fourth album *Barafundle* (1997) after the beach.

Dan yr Ogof

It sounds like the plot from an Indiana Jones film. Or maybe the latest instalment in the Jurassic Park series. In 1912, two intrepid explorers went on an expedition in search of the source of a magical water supply. Armed with little more than a few candles, a coracle, and a gun, the Morgan brothers – farmers Tommy and Jeff – ended up stumbling across what is now said to be the largest natural showcaves complex in northern Europe.

Dan yr Ogof, the National Showcaves Centre in Abercraf, contains centuries of ancient history, from human bones to stalagmites and stalactites. If that wasn't enough, the upper Swansea Valley tourist attraction is also potentially the largest dinosaur park in the world, with more than 250 life-sized prehistoric monsters on its grounds.

Dinosaur sculptures at Dan yr Ogof. © *Nilfanion (Wikimedia, CC BY-SA 4.0)*

Afan Forest Park

Afan Forest Park attracts athletic visitors from around the world to tackle the Afan Valley's many mountain biking and walking trails. Often referred to by its traditional name Afan Argoed, the forest park covers 48 square miles of greenery, and was home to the Kanji Wood, a unique Japanese forest in the heart of Port Talbot. Conceived by Clive William Nicol, an author and environmentalist from Neath who moved to Japan in the 1960s, the forest park was twinned with a woodland area near Nicol's new home in Nagano. This meant that not only was there a little bit of Japan in the form of trees and sculptures in Wales, but Japan had an a little bit of Wales with its own Afan Woodland.

Afan Forest Park's walks include nine waymarked structured routes which range from a quick thirty-minute ramble to a day's exploring. But for a lot of people, its all about the mountain bike trails. Possibly the most famous is the Penhydd Trail, a looping trail which was originally created by local biking enthusiasts, and which has inspired many of its additional trails. These include the cliff-top Wall Trail, and for a real challenge with great views, the 28-mile Skyline Trail.

The park also has a unique outdoor woodland theatre called Theatre Tymaen, which can stage productions in an amphitheatre-like setting. Some of the nearby accommodation houses could also be described as mini-landmarks, having been designed to resemble Swiss cottages.

Merthyr Mawr National Nature Reserve

The village of Merthyr Mawr in Bridgend has a fantastic claim to fame: it is home to the second-highest sand dunes in Europe, with only France's famous Dune of Pilat going one better. Dubbed the 'south Wales Sahara', they can be found in the Merthyr Mawr Nature Reserve, which spans an area of around 800 acres, with the the 60m Big Dipper at its peak.

An SSSI cared for by Natural Resources Wales, the nature reserve is home to diverse plants and wildlife, such as the rare great green bush-cricket and the *Glocianus Pilosellus* weevil. The ruins of Candleston Castle, a fourteenth-century stone manor house, can be found less than a mile away on the edge of the sands.

The series of dunes which make up the nature reserve once ran all the way along the south Wales coast, from the Gower Peninsula in the west to Ogmore in the east, and were connected to this book's next landmark, Kenfig Pool National Nature Reserve.

Did You Know ...

The Merthyr Mawr dunes doubled up as the Arabian desert in the Academy Award-winning film *Lawrence of Arabia* (1962) starring Peter O'Toole.

Kenfig Pool National Nature Reserve
While they might not reach quite the same heights as those at Merthyr Mawr, Kenfig Pool National Nature Reserve also has an impressive range of ancient sand dunes, and it more than makes up for any shortcomings with its own long-lost buried city.

Kenfig Pool itself is a 70-acre freshwater pool which sits on the edge of the dunes, from where you can get a panoramic view of Port Talbot's most prominent industrial landmark, the

Kenfig National Nature Reserve. © *Mick Lobb (Wikimedia, CC BY-SA 2.0)*

steelworks. According to the legends, the pool is bottomless, and you could get sucked into a whirlpool and meet a watery death. Others say that it has a maximum depth of 3.5m.

Another legend claims that it conceals a sunken city, and while this might be fiction, the village of Kenfig does indeed hide a 'lost city', the remains of which are buried beneath the sands of the nature reserve. The ruins of Kenfig Castle, which can be seen poking out of the dunes at Kenfig Burrows, mark the spot where people would have originally settled in the village. They were forced to move further inland when the sand began to advance towards their homes, and what remained was wiped out entirely in 1607 by the 'great storm', a suspected tsunami in the Bristol Channel. Not only did it strike Kenfig, but many other places in Wales in the counties of Glamorgan, Pembrokeshire, Monmouthshire and Cardiff, as well as parts of England. Now a designated SSSI, it is a haven for birdwatchers, with its own bird hides from where the uncommon bittern bird can be seen in winter. Rare plants include the fen orchid.

Cosmeston Lakes Country Park

Cosmeston Lakes Country Park in Penarth was, from the late nineteenth century to the late 1960s, a leading limestone quarry. Many of the old industrial sites have since been transformed beyond recognition, and the cement works it used to supply is now the Cosmeston housing estate opposite. The only real factory building remaining from this period is the nearby Harvester restaurant.

The area in the Vale of Glamorgan was redeveloped in the 1970s into its current guise as a picturesque country park. Its two most distinctive features, a pair of lakes which are populated by wild fowl, were actually areas of land excavated during its time as a works, which naturally filled with water. Parts of the park are SSSIs.

A 'mile road' footpath leads around the local nature reserve, and over the watery areas which can be crossed by bridge. A highlight is the Cosmeston Medieval Village, a recreation of a fourteenth-century village that was discovered while developing the grounds. It is now a hotspot for historical re-enactments, with tents, costumes, and opposing sides doing battle in a traditional setting.

6

COASTAL TREASURES

In 2012, Wales became the first country in the world to establish a public footpath route along the vast majority of its coastline. The Wales Coast Path (Llwybr Arfordir Cymru) is an epic 870-mile walk, which starts in the south-east in the Monmouthshire town of Chepstow, and winds its way up to the Flintshire town of Queensferry in the north-west.

To make things a bit more manageable, the route can be divided up into eight sections, each with their own individual maps. These are: North Wales Coast and the Dee Estuary (68 miles); Isle of Anglesey (132 miles); Menai, Llŷn and Meirionnydd (189 miles); Ceredigion (72 miles); Pembrokeshire (186 miles); Carmarthenshire (68 miles); Gower and Swansea Bay (71 miles); and south Wales Coast and Severn Estuary (97 miles). Anyone in search of landmarks along the country's coast, from the Victorian piers to the magical islands, can follow one of these simple routes.

Did You Know ...

By combining the Wales Coast Path with the Offa's Dyke Path, which runs along the English border, you could walk around almost the entire country in just two routes. But it might take some time – the combined distance would be 1,030 miles.

Mwnt. © *Dickelbers (Wikimedia, CC BY-SA 3.0)*

COVES AND BEACHES

Mwnt Beach
The National Trust's Mwnt Beach in the small Ceredigion community of Mwnt is an often overlooked hidden gem. The secluded cove is surrounded by the sea, where dolphins and porpoises can be seen in Cardigan Bay. To really take in its beauty, head to the top of Foel y Mwnt, a 76m-high cone-shaped hill which lends its name to the sands below.

Mwnt has long been a holy site, and was visited by pilgrims en route to more famous destinations like Bardsey Island. Its Holy Cross church (Eglwys y Grog) is a Grade I listed building which is thought to date from the fourteenth century, although the site itself could be centuries older, having been built as a chapel of ease for visiting medieval sailors who couldn't easily reach the main parish church.

Poppit Sands
As the name suggests, Poppit Sands really is all about sand: a seemingly endless stretch of golden, flowing, dry sand. A mile and a half away from the village of St Dogmaels, it is Pembrokeshire's

most northerly beach, and marks the start (or the end, depending on your direction) of the Pembrokeshire Coast Path.

Sitting at the mouth of the Teifi Estuary in Cardigan Bay, it offers views across the waves to Cardigan Island, and curves southwards towards the bay of Amroth in Saundersfoot. With low dunes leading the way to its beach, the western side is the rockier area, and where the dunes have some uncommon plants growing in them, such as the bee orchid. As with other landmarks in the area, grey seals, bottlenose dolphins and porpoises can be seen in the water in the warmer months, and you'll often find surfers hitting the waves.

Cwm yr Eglwys

Cwm yr Eglwys is a secluded sandy cove in the village of Dinas in Pembrokeshire. And its name, which translates as the Valley of the Church, offers a clue as to the real landmark to be found there.

On the Dinas Island peninsula stands the remains of the church of St Brynach, battered over the centuries by storms and the sea. The ruins were partially pulled down in the late nineteenth century, but the atmospheric west wall still remains, surrounded by many of its original gravestones.

The peninsula is cared for by the National Trust, and forms a part of the Pembrokeshire Coast National Park. It reaches a height of 142m at Dinas Head, from where landmarks to look out for include the Strumble Head Lighthouse on the Strumble Head headland in the distance.

The Blue Lagoon

The Blue Lagoon in Abereiddi, which is also spelled Abereiddy in English, is world famous with watersport fans. The rocky lagoon in the Pembrokeshire hamlet is a favourite for coasteering and rock climbing, and has played host to the Red Bull Cliff Diving World Series on several occasions, which sees daredevil divers hurl themselves 27m into the waters below.

The Blue Lagoon takes its name from a former slate quarry which was in use until the early twentieth century; the remains of the workers' homes and buildings can be seen and explored in the area. The lagoon itself was created when the passage linking the sea to the quarry was broken, flooding the old works.

The quarry has given the sand a unique dark shade, while the water has a green tinge, despite the blue name.

Newgale Beach

The first thing which strikes anyone who visits Newgale beach for the first time is its size – the beach looks huge, with more than 2 miles of sandy beach lined with pebbles strecthing as far as the eye can see. One of Pembrokeshire's most well-known beaches, it is perfect for walking along, or taking to the water to challenge its 'big surf'. For explorers, it also leads to other more secluded bays, rock pools and coves along the Pembrokeshire Coast Path, with a highlight being a cave which can be walked through at Maidenhall Point on the southern end.

Whitesands Bay

A landmark for surfers, Whitesands Bay is said to be one of the most popular surfing spots in the UK. Just a mile from St David's Head in Pembrokeshire, its Welsh name Porthmawr means big harbour.

It is a place of archaeological treasures; if you time it right, you can just about see the forest which is submerged beneath the waves jutting out from the sand. The best times to see the ancient tree stumps is said to be during a low tide following a storm.

Whitesands Bay. © *Nilfanion (Wikimedia, CC BY-SA 4.0)*

Whitesands Bay sits in the shadow of the imposing Carn Llidi, a 181m-high hill which is home to even more historical finds, including two potential neolithic burial chambers. Also sitting above the bay is Tŷ Gwyn, a farmhouse and former monastery which, according to a local legend, is where Wales's patron saint St David was schooled.

In the fifth century another patron saint, this time St Patrick, is said to have set sail from the bay following a vision which instructed him to convert the Irish to Christianity. A chapel was dedicated to him nearby, a pilgrimage point on the trail to St David's Cathedral, and a stone marking the site can be found below a mound reading:

> Underneath lies a chapel dedicated to St Patrick built 6th–10th Century. Excavated 1924.

Pendine Sands

Pendine Sands in Carmarthenshire is famous not only for being a glorious stretch of sand, but also as an early destination for British motorcar racing. It was also the scene of one of the greatest tragedies in Welsh sport.

Stretching for 7 miles from Gilman Point to Laugharne Sands, the beach has been in the care of the Ministry of Defence since the Second World War, when they used it as a firing range.

In the early twentieth century, the Carmarthen Bay beach was favoured by motoring enthusiasts as it offered a flatter and sturdier surface on which to attempt to break speed limits. The land speed record was broken four times on the beach, first by Englishman Sir Malcolm Campbell in 1924, and then by Welshman J.G. Parry-Thomas from Wrexham. The pair jostled for the title, and it was while attempting to beat Campbell's 174.22mph in 1927 that Parry-Thomas, while travelling close to 170mph, was involved in a fatal crash. His record-breaking car Babs, which he had built himself, was buried in the nearby sand dunes, until it was excavated and restored by Owen Wyn Owen in 1967. It can usually be seen on display at Pendine Museum of Speed during the summer months.

The beach is still used for motoring events and land speed attempts today. Some of the more well-publicised include motorbike racer Guy Martin, who broke the 'UK speed record for a bicycle ridden in the slipstream of another vehicle' for his Channel 4 TV series in 2013. Also for a TV show, in 2015 actor Idris Elba broke Sir Malcolm Campbell's 'Flying Mile' record in a Bentley Continental GT Speed for his Discovery Channel series, hitting a top speed of 180.361mph.

Cefn Sidan

Cefn Sidan, which means 'silky back' in Welsh, is a golden beach which has been described as one of the 'best beaches in Europe', and even compared to those in California by some. The first Welsh beach to receive the Blue Flag award for its high standards, it stretches for 8 miles between Burry Port and Kidwelly, and forms a part of Pembrey Country Park.

The Carmarthenshire park is also home to 500 acres of green parkland, and has its own miniature railway and ski slope.

Jackson's Bay

Jackson's Bay is something of a secret beach when compared to the more well-known places in this book, and is that much better because of it. A modest, sandy bay tucked away in Barry Island in the Vale of Glamorgan, it can found near the town's lifeboat station in the port and harbour. It is 170m long and the enclosed cliff-backed cove slopes down towards the ocean, from where you can look out towards the Bristol Channel.

On the eastern side is a harbour wall with a lighthouse at the end, on the other side of which are the harbour's boats. On the western side is Nell's Point, where the first National Coastwatch Institution station to be established in Wales keep an eye on the busy waters.

The seaside resort is probably best known for Barry Island Pleasure Park, an amusement park which dates back to Victorian times. Its popularity was bolstered in more recent times thanks to the success of BBC sitcom *Gavin & Stacey*, and there are occasional bus tours available which take in some of the the locations featured in the show.

Eglwys Santes Dwynwen, Llanddwyn Island. © *TuK Bassler (Wikimedia, CC BY-SA 4.0)*

ISLANDS AND PENINSULAS

Ynys Llanddwyn
Ynys Llanddwyn, or Llanddwyn Island in English, near the town of Newborough was the home of Wales's patron saint of love. The island off Anglesey's west coast takes its names from Santes (St) Dwynwen, a Welsh saint whose feast day on 25 January is celebrated in much the same way as St Valentine's, with cards, chocolates, and the added Welsh twist of love spoons.

Legend has it that the fifth-century saint forsook love for herself in order to bring it to others. After falling for the unattainable suitor Maelon Dafodrill, she prayed to have all thoughts of her beloved removed. Answering her plea, an angel arrived with a potion which not only erased Dafodrill from her memory, but froze him into a block of ice. When God granted Dwynwen three wishes, her first was to thaw her former sweetheart from his icy prison; her second was to ask God to take care of all true lovers; and her third was that she would remain unmarried for the rest of her life.

The reason for the final wish was to allow her to devote her life to God's service, taking the nun's habit on Ynys Llanddwyn where the remains of her church can be seen. A pilgrimage destination, a newer church was built on the site of the original in the sixteenth century. Other religious landmarks on the island include two prominent crosses which cut a dramatic shape in the skyline. Erected by the island's then-owner F.G. Wynn in the early twentieth century, one is a decorative Celtic cross with inscriptions in English on one side and Welsh on the other. The second is a plain Christian cross in memory of Santes Dwynwen herself.

The island is connected to the mainland but can become cut off for hours at a time during high tides. The route to the island contains large pillow lavas in the sand, which are rocky lava formations shaped like pillows.

The Great Orme

The Great Orme is said to take its name from the Viking word for a sea monster. The striking peninsula juts into the sea, and was thought to resemble the head of a mythological creature, with the land forming its body. Not far from Llandudno, it is also known as Great Orme's Head and Y Gogarth or Pen y Gogarth in Welsh. The limestone headland rises 207m out of the ocean, and could be more than 350 million years old. This 'mini island' is home to the Great Orme Country Park, which can be reached on foot or by car, but a more traditional and scenic way of arriving at the summit is by cable car, or on board the Great Orme Tramway.

Copper mining began on the Great Orme in the Bronze Age, when stone tools were used to carve out Malachite ore. The working Great Orme Bronze Age Mines, which is said to be the world's largest Bronze Age mine, can be visited by the public.

A lot of water would have been needed for the mine, and the area is dotted with natural wells. This includes Ffynnon Llech inside the hard-to-access cave Ogof Llech, where the sixth-century monk St Tudno is said to have lived as a hermit. In the Middle Ages there were three townships on the Great Orme, and the saint established the first parish church in Cyngreawdr. While no trace of the original church remains, a wall from its twelfth-century replacement bearing his name still stands. The church was extended in the fifteenth century, and the adjoining graveyard was added during the Victorian era. The other townships were Y Gogarth, where the remains of the Bishop of Bangor's thirteenth-century palace can be seen, and Yn Wyddfid, which boomed in size in the eighteenth century thanks to the copper mines reopening.

Half of the headland is now farmland, and includes the National Trust's Parc Farm, where a farmhouse continues the traditional method of sheep-herding, and where rare plants like the spiked speedwell are preserved. It is a designated Heritage Coast, SAC, and an SSSI, and rare wildlife includes the silver-studded blue, a species of butterfly which is unique to the area, the rare red-billed chough birds, and the Kashmir goats which roam wild.

A smaller limestone headland called Little Orme can also be found in Llandudno Bay.

Bardsey Island
Gwynedd's 'Isle of Twenty Thousand Saints' didn't get its nickname for nothing.

A site steeped in spirituality, the island in Snowdonia National Park is said to be the final resting place of 20,000 saints, and if that wasn't enough, King Arthur and his faithful magician Merlin are also said to be buried there. The mile-long, 0.6 mile wide island is 2 miles out to sea from the end of the Llŷn Peninsula, and is also known as 'The Island of the Tides', a translation of its Welsh name, Ynys Enlli. Bardsey Island itself means 'The Island of the Bards', which could be a nod to Wales's literary heritage, or derived from the Viking language.

Religious tourists have long made pilgrimages to the island, which was at one point so important that it was said to nearly rival Rome as a destination, with two or three trips to Bardsey said to be the equivalent of one to the headquarters. Its monastery is seen as a highlight; it was founded by its abbot St Cadfan, a sixth-century Breton nobleman who had previously established the church in nearby Tywyn.

Bardsey Island is a National Nature Reserve and SSSI. The oldest remaining building from its time as a pilgrimage hotspot is the tower from St Mary's Abbey, which dates from the thirteenth century. Going back even further, the remains of six round huts and a wall which could be up to 3,000 years old can be seen on the Mynydd Enlli mountain.

The island is also a bird-watching destination; Bardsey Bird and Field Observatory was founded in the 1950s from which to observe the winged visitors, and it is best known for its Manx shearwaters, which breed in large numbers – there can be as many as 16,000 on the island, staying safely away from mainland predators.

Sea life can be found by looking down into the rock pools, while out in the waters you might catch a glimpse of the harbour porpoises, the Risso's dolphin or a grey seal. When it comes to important plants, the island is home to the western clover herb, the small adder's tongue fern and rock sea-lavender.

The Afal Enlli (Bardsey Apple) is said to be the rarest apple in the world, and its mother tree, which is thought to be the only remaining apple tree from the island's ancient monastery, grows on the side of a nineteenth-century house called Plas Bach. According to one legend, the tree is known as Merlin's Apple, and the magician is said to be buried, or sleeping at least, in a cave or a glass castle nearby. A similar tale is told about King Arthur, who is lying in wait for the country's darkest hour to return, and whose ship is now at the bottom of the Bardsey Sound. Bardsey Island could even be Avalon, the island from Arthurian legend.

Shell Island

Shell Island is the ideal landmark if you're looking for – you guessed it – shells. It is about 2.5 miles west of Llanbedr, and more than 200 different kinds of unusual seashells can be found washed up on its sands. Once the home of an ancient settlement, it is also known as Mochras, and is a part of the Snowdonia National Park. It dates from 1819, when Gwynedd's River Artro was redirected by the Earl of Winchilsea to allow for greater access for slate shipments from the nearby works.

It has many varieties of wild flowers, including thirteen species of wild orchid which grow throughout the year, and is a go-to place for wild camping, with neighbours given a wide berth from each other for that feeling of being alone with nature. Its picturesque harbour is a landmark for anglers, or those who just want to watch the boats sail in.

Cardigan Island

Cardigan Island (Ynys Aberteifi), the 'uninhabited island', is the place to go and see wildlife – if not necessarily people. But while the island might have a population of zero, there is evidence that humans were once busy there with ancient finds including a turf wall thought be a part of an old Christian site. It is 200m off the coast of Gwbert, a hamlet in Ceredigion, and is only accessible by boat, which can be caught from Gwbert or nearby Cardigan. Covering an area of 38 acres, it is cared for by the Wildlife Trust of South and West Wales, and some of the marine wildlife in its waters include bottlenose dolphins and a colony of grey seals who populate the island's caves.

Inland are the wild Soay sheep, which originally hail from Scotland's Soay island and were introduced in the 1940s, while birdwatchers can spot thousands of nesting birds, with guillemots, choughs and cormorants among those who flock to the island. For land-lovers who prefer not to cross the water, there are some good vantage points to view the island from afar, such as Cardigan Island Farm Park or the Cemaes Head nature reserve.

Skomer Island

There are several islands to explore off the coast of Pembrokeshire, but Skomer Island (Ynys Sgomer) can really be described as a landmark hunter's paradise.

From heritage to wildlife it has the lot, and the protection to prove it: a large part of the island is a designated ancient monument, its waters are a marine nature reserve, and its also an SSSI, a Special Protection Area and a National Nature Reserve.

Surrounded by three islets, Mew Stone, Midland Isle and Garland Stone, it covers an area of 1.13 square miles and is blanketed by bluebells in the spring. It is accessible by boat from Martin's Haven, a small pebble-covered bay which falls within the Skomer Marine Conservation Zone; once you arrive on land the addition of a hostel means that you can now spend the night there.

Puffin on Skomer Island off the Welsh coast. © *S A Hooper (Wikimedia, CC BY 2.0)*

Among the wildlife around the island are dolphins, grey seals and harbour porpoises, while inland you might see the unique Skomer vole, a bank vole which is not found anywhere else in the world. When it comes to birds, nearly half of the world's population of Manx shearwaters are said to nest on the island, and it is probably best known for its colony of Atlantic puffins, with a staggering 10,000 pairs estimated to be breeding there. Its highest point is Gorse Hill, which stands at 79m above sea level, and it also has its fair share of archaeological landmarks, including ancient stones and houses.

Ramsey Island

Ramsey Island off the coast of St David's peninsula is a rugged landmark which can be accessed by boat. The island's Welsh name, Ynys Dewi, refers to St David, or Dewi Sant. In the sixth century it was home to St Justinian of Ramsey Island, a Breton nobleman, who was given the role of Abbot of St David's

Cathedral by Wales's patron saint. According to the legend, he relocated to Ramsey Island in search of a stricter and more spiritual way of life. Living life as a hermit, he was joined by some of his fellow monks, but they struggled to adhere to his rigorous form of piety. So the brothers ended up enacting their revenge in the most gruesome of ways: they decapitated their former abbot. At that point St Justinian is said to have gathered up his own head and walked across the ocean to the chapel of St Justinian where he was buried.

The island is less than 2 miles long, and the best way to explore it is to walk the 3.5-mile trail around it. For panoramic views, head to the summits of Carn Ysgubor and the island's highest point, Carnllundain, a listed HuMP (Hundred Metre Prominence) with an elevation of 136m.

The island is an RSPB nature reserve, and birds of prey on the island include peregrines and buzzards. The caves serve as homes for the island's other main inhabitants, the seals; in the autumn, up to 400 pups can be born here.

A popular spot with extreme sports fans is the unusually named The Bitches; a series of rocks between the island and the coast where treacherous whirlpools can form, they create fast waves when the tide passes through. The island is also a site of archaeological interest, with discoveries including round barrows and a promontory fort thought to date from the Bronze Age.

To the west of Ramsey Island are the Bishops and Clerks, a group of rocks and four islets. South Bishop Lighthouse, which was designed by James Walker and built in 1839, stands on Emsger, the largest of the islets.

COASTAL LANDMARKS

Aberaeron
When it comes to taking a break along the Welsh coast, seaside resorts don't come much more picturesque than Aberaeron in Ceredigion. Famed for its food and drink, its seafood and honey are a speciality, with the honey making its way into the tourists' favourite honey ice cream.

A traditional fishing port along the Ceredigion Coast Path, Aberaeron's harbour dates from the early nineteenth century, and while it might have once welcomed giant steamships into port, it now houses smaller boats bobbing on the waves. The shoreline and its pebbly beaches can be walked along, while a postcard-perfect landmark in the Georgian town itself are the rows of brightly coloured houses.

Pembroke Dockyard
Pembroke Dockyard is home to more than 100 fascinating listed buildings. Founded in 1814 in Paterchurch, or as we now know it, the town of Pembroke Dock, the dockyard was established by the Royal Navy, and was called Pater Yard for its first few years. It remained in operation and produced around 260 ships until the end of the First World War, after which the Royal Air Force based themselves at the site in the 1930s.

Its oldest landmark is the Paterchurch Tower, a medieval Grade I listed building which once stood at the centre of a large estate. Named after the wealthy de Paterchurch landowners, the fortified tower is 10.7m high and is assumed to have been a peel tower, used for observational purposes.

Did You Know …

When a life-sized Millennium Falcon was needed for the *Star Wars* sequel *The Empire Strikes Back* (1980), it was assembled at a top secret location in Pembroke Dock. Measuring 21m in diameter and weighing 23 tonnes, Han Solo's spaceship was made in Wales.

Witches' Cauldron
The Witches' Cauldron – or Pwll y Wrach, which means Pool of the Witch – is a Pembrokeshire cave famous for its unusual bright green water. Far from being the easiest of landmarks to access, you'll have to time your visit just right, but it's more than worth the extra bit of effort.

The best way to experience the fairytale-like cave is by kayak. Tucked away near Ceibwr Bay, there are secret tunnels which can only be explored by boat, with features such as a waterfall

Green Bridge of Wales. © *JKMMX (Wikimedia, CC BY-SA 3.0)*

to be discovered inside the collapsed cave. But the entrance to the cave can be easily missed, so keep your eyes peeled.

You can also walk to the Witches' Cauldron along the Wales Coastal Path, but not during the autumn months when the seals are giving birth. Sadly, those on foot will not have the same vantage point as those on the water.

The Green Bridge of Wales

Inside the Castlemartin Training Area, 6,000 acres of Ministry of Defence-owned land by Stack Rocks, is one of Pembrokeshire's greatest natural treasures, a limestone arch known as the Green Bridge of Wales.

Found within the boundaries of the Pembrokeshire Coast National Park, the area is rich in carboniferous limestone, and erosion from the sea has resulted in the formation of caves and spaces. Taking its name from the green plant life which covers its arch, the Green Bridge of Wales is said to be the biggest natural arch in the UK, standing 24m tall and more than 20m wide.

The area is an SSSI, a Special Protected Area, and an SAC, and is popular with climbers, although nesting birds means that getting hands-on with the rocks isn't always allowed.

A viewing platform nearby is an easier way of observing the bridge, which leads out towards the ocean waves and the rocks below.

Did You Know ...

Other nearby carboniferous limestone attractions which have been formed due to erosion are Huntsman's Leap, a steep chasm also in the training area, and Elegug Stacks, two staggering pillars of rock which burst from the water.

Tenby Harbour
The Welsh name for the Pembrokeshire town of Tenby is Dinbych-y-pysgod, which translates as the more exotic-sounding 'fortlet of the fish'. One of the Georgian town's highlights is its gateway to the sea, a boat-lined harbour which is sandwiched between the old town and Castle Hill. This is where a tower, the final remains of a twelfth-century Norman castle, can be found.

The harbour has its own mini-beach, and is used at times as an amphitheatre-like area for outdoor performances. It is also where boats set off to explore some of this book's island landmarks, such as Caldey Island.

There are 372 listed places in the town, including the Grade I medieval town walls, a defensive structure dating from the thirteenth century; the National Trust's Tudor Merchant's House, a preserved fifteenth-century stone house and the oldest house in Tenby; and St Mary's Church, the majority of which also dates from the fifteenth century, with a wagon roof in the thirteenth-century chancel covered with architectural bosses.

Did You Know ...

Tenby is an artistic town bustling with crafts and painting. J.M.W. Turner once visited to paint its north shore, and leading twentieth-century Welsh painter Augustus John was born there.

Porthcawl
Porthcawl is the embodiment of the traditional notion of a British seaside holiday. From donkey rides on the beach

to coin-sliding amusement arcades, all can be found in the Bridgend town.

There are seven sandy beaches in the area, the most popular with tourists being Trecco Bay, Rest Bay and Sandy Bay. The town's promenade runs along the seafront, and landmarks along the way include the Grand Pavilion theatre, and the Porthcawl Lifeboat Station in the Harbour Quarter. This leads on to Porthcawl Pier, at the end of which is the lighthouse dating from 1860. The Jennings Building is a Grade II listed warehouse which has been restored as a dining place with sea views. Built in 1832, it is said to be the country's 'oldest maritime warehouse'.

The biggest landmark in Porthcawl, however, would have to be Coney Beach Pleasure Park. It originally opened in 1920, and was influenced by New York's famous Coney Island. It is one of the few remaining seaside fun fairs where you can ride a ghost train while eating candy floss, or have a cone of chips before popping on a roller coaster.

LIGHTHOUSES

South Stack Lighthouse

There's no shortage of landmarks on the Isle of Anglesey, but South Stack lighthouse must rank as one of the island's finest attractions. Although you'll have to like steep walks to reach it – the lighthouse trail starts with a downward trek of 400 steps (390 stone and 10 metal), before crossing a high chasm on a bridge in order to arrive at the small islet which sticks out into the Irish Sea.

The lighthouse stands 28m tall on the rocky South Stack island off Holy Island, and dates back to 1808 when Trinity House constructed it in nine short months using stone mainly quarried from the island itself. The creation of the lighthouse was given the go-ahead following a heated campaign by Captain Hugh Evans, who was determined to reduce the number of shipwrecks in the area. An iron suspension bridge inspired by the nearby Menai Bridge was added in 1827, with the current bridge, a stronger crossing assembled around the previous incarnation, built in the late 1990s.

The area is home to an RSPB nature reserve, South Stack Cliffs Nature Reserve, with thousands of birds including guillemots, razorbills and the area's famous puffins flocking there in spring to nest.

For a good view of the lighthouse itself, and a panoramic view of the surrounding area, head to nearby Elin's Tower, a castellated tower which was once used as a summer house and is now run by the RSPB.

Did You Know ...

The cover photo to Roxy Music's 1975 album *Siren* features frontman Bryan Ferry's then-girlfriend Jerry Hall on the rocks near South Stack.

Point of Ayr Lighthouse

The Point of Ayr lighthouse near the village of Talacre in Flintshire could be the most wonderfully located privately owned property in Wales. Also known as the Talacre lighthouse due to its location

Point of Ayr Lighthouse. © *Mark Warren 1973 (Wikimedia, CC BY-SA 4.0)*

on the village's beach, the Grade II listed building is an 18m-tall brick lighthouse which stands on the sand itself. Originally built in 1776 to guide ships into the River Dee estuary, it was rebuilt in 1844, but has been out of use since 1883.

Point of Ayr itself is the site of the RSPB's Dee Estuary Nature Reserve, with many species flocking to the area throughout the year, including little terns and ringed plovers. It also lies in the Gronant and Talacre Dunes SSSI.

Possibly thanks to its remote location, the lighthouse has been the scene of many a ghost sighting over the years, with holidaymakers experiencing feelings of unease nearby, and in some cases capturing what they say is photographic evidence of a spirit. One of the more popular theories is that it is haunted by an old lighthouse keeper who watches from the balcony, and that his footprints have been seen in the sand outside.

Nash Point Lighthouse

Nash Point lighthouse can be found on the cliffs of Nash Point beach and headland in the Vale of Glamorgan. Work began on the 37m-tall stone tower in 1831, soon after fifty people lost their lives in the the wreck of the *Frolic* in its waters. Designed by James Walker for Trinity House, it was lit a year later.

The lighthouse, a Grade II listed building, was de-manned in 1998, and now serves as a tourist attraction. Its famous siren-like foghorn can be heard up to 20 miles away, and is occasionally sounded for the benefit of visitors.

Many fossils have been found in the the rocks on the Monknash Coast, which is also home to Nash Point Camp, an ancient Iron Age area with a hill fort, barrows and burial sites. Outside of the lighthouse, the surrounding meadow is an SSSI, home to birds and the rare spiky *Cirsium tuberosum* thistle.

Did You Know ...

Just north from the lighthouse is a wrecked BP tanker, which hit the rocks in 1962 and remains submerged. At low tide you might catch a glimpse of it.

PIERS

Llandudno Pier

Nothing quite says seaside holiday like a traditional Victorian pier lined with shops and bars. And Llandudno Pier isn't just any old pier – it's the longest in Wales, and the fifth-longest in England and Wales. The Grade II* listed pier stretches 700m out into the water, at the end of which is a landing stage for setting off into deep water.

When it began life in 1858 it was a much shorter 74m wooden pier, which suffered considerable damage during the Royal Charter Storm of 1859. The current iron pier replaced it in 1877, with extensions and additions added throughout the nineteenth century.

Garth Pier

Garth Pier in Bangor is the second-longest pier in Wales, behind previous landmark Llandudno Pier. The iron pier in the

Llandudno Pier. © *Gary Beale (Wikimedia, CC BY-SA 4.0)*

Gwynedd city was opened in the late nineteenth century, and reaches 460m out into the Menai Strait. It is still with us today thanks to a local campaign which overturned the decision to have it demolished in the 1970s, and saw it awarded Grade II listed status.

It is a good spot for bird watchers; a range of seabirds can be observed at close distance in the shallow waters.

Mumbles Pier
Mumbles Pier is a landmark in a village which could be described as a landmark in itself. The seaside beauty spot's unusual name, which is spelled Mwmbwls in Welsh, has nothing to do with mumbling your words, but is so-called because its two islands are said to resemble a pair of breasts, and could derive from the French *mamelle*, or the Latin *mamucium*.

The pier stands at the end of Swansea's promenade, which runs along Swansea Bay towards Gower. When it first opened in 1898 it also marked the end of the Swansea and Mumbles Railway, the 'world's first passenger carrying railway', which closed in 1960.

The roughly 250m-long Victorian pier is now a Grade II listed building, and over the years has expanded to meet the demands of tourism. On the pier itself are two familiar – to the people of Swansea, at least – faces: the Mumbles Pier monkey, and the Mumbles Pier red dragon, a pair of children's sculptures that crop up in countless tourist snaps and postcards.

The Royal National Lifeboat Institution has a lifeboat station at the end of the pier, from where Mumbles lighthouse can be seen on the islands off Mumbles Head. Completed in 1794, the 17m-tall landmark has evolved with the times, and is now a solar-powered beacon.

A quirky landmark nearby is the Mumbles Big Apple, a seasonal retail outlet in the shape of a giant fruit just above the pier.

7

A LAND OF CASTLES

There are more castles in Wales per square mile than any other country in the world, and when it comes to Welsh landmarks, they don't get much more iconic than the estimated 600 – yes, 600 – which are said to cover the land. Of those, around 100 are still standing, while the remaining 500 or so have left clues of their existence in the form of overgrown ditches and strategically placed mounds.

Some of the more spectacular castles, such as Caernarfon, Harlech, Conwy and Beaumaris, collectively known as The Castles and Town Walls of King Edward in Gwynedd, can be read about in the UNESCO World Heritage Site chapter above.

But what of the countless others? Starting in the north and working our way down south, here is a selection of Wales's landmark fortresses.

CRICCIETH CASTLE

Criccieth Castle is a native Welsh castle perched on the headland overlooking the town of Criccieth in Gwynedd. It occupies an impressive spot, surrounded by the waters of the Tremadog Bay inlet in Cardigan Bay, with beaches of sand and pebbles on either side. Presumed to have been built by Welsh ruler Llywelyn the Great (Llywelyn Fawr), it was overthrown and upgraded by Edward I, and later laid siege to by the forces of Madog ap Llywelyn. Captured and damaged by the forces of Owain Glyndŵr during his rebellion, it is now cared for by Cadw.

Work began on the castle in the first half of the thirteenth century, and its most dominant feature remains its two large

Criccieth. © *Tanya Dedyukhina (Wikimedia, CC BY 3.0)*

defensive gatehouse towers, which were designed in the apsidal stretched 'D' shape. There is some rare decorative work in the gatehouse, where a figure of a crucified Christ was found, and is now a part of the collection of National Museum Wales. Criccieth is one of a series of Welsh castles which was painted by J.M.W. Turner.

DOLBADARN CASTLE

Dolbadarn Castle is one of Llywelyn the Great's thirteenth-century fortifications, and was the ideal place to station his troops above Llyn Padarn lake on Snowdonia's Llanberis Pass. At 15m tall, it was just as much a show of power as it was strategically important, but after being captured by Edward I it fell into ruin and is now cared for by Cadw.

The Grade I listed Gwynedd castle is dwarfed by its impressive Welsh round tower, which has a series of chambers inside and is surrounded by a stone keep. It is also another of the castles painted by J.M.W. Turner.

PENRHYN CASTLE

Penrhyn Castle is a 'mock' fantasy castle designed in the first half of the nineteenth century by architect to royalty Thomas Hooper. But the country house's history can be traced back to the Middle Ages, when it began life as the manor house of legendary Welsh warrior Ednyfed Fychan. It was later fortified and reconstructed over the centuries.

Within touching distance of the Gwynedd village of Llandygai, the castle is now a National Trust property, and one original feature remaining from Hooper's Norman re-imagining is the spiral staircase. It also houses an impressive collection of art from the likes of Canaletto, Carl Haag, and Welsh landscape pioneer Richard Wilson. Until 2015, it could lay claim to owning Rembrandt's portrait of Catharina Hooghsaet, which was sold by Sotheby's to a private collector for £35 million.

Outside, Penrhyn Castle has a walled area housing large gardens and the Penrhyn Castle Railway Museum.

DOLWYDDELAN CASTLE

The thirteenth-century Dolwyddelan Castle cuts a striking, if solitary, figure in the Conwy landscape. Along with Dolbadarn Castle and Castell Prysor, it formed one of Llywelyn the Great's trio of Snowdonian fortresses, serving as a guard post along a main route into the north. It was in the care of his grandson Llywelyn ap Gruffudd when Edward I's invading army captured it in 1283. Modified and repaired over the centuries, the Grade I listed building was restored by the Victorians in the nineteenth century, and is now in the care of Cadw. Along with its historical importance, it is worth a visit for the views alone.

RHUDDLAN CASTLE

Rhuddlan Castle in the Denbighshire town of Rhuddlan is where Edward I issued the Statute of Rhuddlan, or Statutes of Wales, which imposed English common law on the Welsh. One of the

Rhuddlan Castle. © *Jonny Williams (Wikimedia, CC BY-SA 2.0)*

'iron ring' of castles, Edward made it his Welsh home for a short period, and it is where his daughter Elizabeth of Rhuddlan is assumed to have been born.

The construction of the concentric castle was the first to be directed by the 'master architect' James of St George, and was completed in 1282. Managed by Cadw, the Grade I listed building's most impressive features are the walls and twin towers which border the entrances and defend the inner ward.

BODELWYDDAN CASTLE

Bodelwyddan Castle is a Grade II* listed manor house near the village of Bodelwyddan in Denbighshire. Surrounded by gardens and parkland, the building dates from the second half of the fifteenth century, but was heavily reconstructed and extended in the early 1830s by Sir John Hay Williams, a descendant of House of Commons speaker Sir William Williams, who bought the property in the late seventeenth century. Looking to put his own stamp on the old castle, he hired Joseph Hansom, of Hansom cab fame, and Edward Welch from Flintshire, to work their magic.

During the First World War it served as a hospital and training ground, and a network of trenches from the period still remain. Following a spell as a school, it became the property of Clwyd County Council in 1980, who employed architect Roderick Gradidge to restore the castle's Victorian look. After a partnership with the National Portrait Gallery and the Royal Academy of Arts was struck, some of their collections were displayed inside.

DENBIGH CASTLE

Denbigh Castle, which overlooks the town in Denbighshire, was built on the site of an old Welsh stronghold held by Dafydd ap Gruffydd. Following Edward I's conquest, the castle was created in two phases. Work began with some of the outer defences and towers, but was halted following its capture during the revolt of Madog ap Llywelyn. It was only after Edward's confidant Henry de Lacy, 3rd Earl of Lincoln, reclaimed the land that the second phase began.

The same mistake wasn't made twice, and this time increased defences were written into the plans. These included more than half a mile of walls around the town, and the imposing three-towered main gateway, behind which was a fortified passageway. The stone used in the second phase was of a different colour, making it distinguishable from the first phase.

Denbigh Castle was the scene of much conflict over the centuries; it was forced to defend itself during Owain Glyndŵr's rebellion and again during the Wars of the Roses. It surrendered after a six-month siege during the English Civil War, after which it housed King Charles I of England for a short time. Abandoned in 1660, it is now managed by Cadw, as are the town walls.

FLINT CASTLE

The castles of Edward I feature heavily in this book, but it all started in the Flintshire town of Flint in 1277, where the invader began to build his 'iron ring' of castles around Wales. Sitting on the border with England, its proximity to the city of Chester made Flint Castle an obvious choice to begin encroaching into the land, and was easy to resupply via the River Dee.

Flint is a square castle with circular towers, and the layout is said to be the only one of its kind in Britain. A unique feature is the donjon or keep, a round corner tower which stands apart from the rest of the castle, which consists of an inner and outer bailey with a drawbridge connecting the two across a surrounding moat. Cared for by Cadw, most of the castle is open to the public, including the distinctive donjon.

Did You Know ...

Flint Castle is one of the few Welsh locations to feature in the works of William Shakespeare. In *Richard II* it is the scene of the title character's capture.

CASTELL DINAS BRÂN

The origins of Castell Dinas Brân castle are patchy at best, but what it lacks in hard historical evidence it more than makes up for in myths and legends. Even the origins of its name are unclear. In English, it has become known as Crow Castle, and it could be a translation of the Welsh for Crow's Fortress.

Sitting on a hilltop overlooking Llangollen and the Dee Valley in Denbighshire, the rectangular fortress is built in a rugged, defensively solid location, backed by a steep drop down its northern side. It is thought to have been created on the site of an Iron Age hill fort from 600 BC by Gruffydd II ap Madog, Lord of Dinas Brân, in the second half of the thirteenth century. It was passed on to his sons, but following Edward I's invasion it fell into ruin.

According to a legend, the castle was the scene of a tragic love story. In the fourteenth century, Myfanwy Fychan of Castell Dinas Brân was the most beautiful girl in Powys – and didn't she know it, stringing along her suitors by making them compose verse and music in her honour. The most talented of them was Hywel ap Einion, a poor bard who showered Myfanwy with words of love. She gave the indication that she loved him in return – until a wealthier suitor turned up. Hywel was left to wander aimlessly, composing words of unrequited love, and his story was immortalised in one of Wales's most hauntingly beautiful songs, 'Myfanwy', composed by Joseph Parry to lyrics by Richard Davies, and first published in 1875.

The castle is now owned by Denbighshire County Council, and is maintained with the help of Cadw.

CHIRK CASTLE

Besides being one of Edward I's 'iron ring' of castles around north Wales, Chirk Castle has played an important role in the arts, and in particular the performing arts, in Wales. Known as Castell y Waun in Welsh, the Grade I listed fortress was built in the town of Chirk because of its strategic position in the Welsh Marches to block entry into the Ceiriog Valley.

Dating from 1295, the castle was bought by Sir Thomas Myddelton in 1593, and remained in the family until 2004. It was during the 1930s that English peer and influential Welsh arts

Chirk Castle with Adam's Tower. © *Prichardson (Wikimedia, public domain)*

supporter Thomas Scott-Ellis, 8th Baron Howard de Walden, relocated to the castle. He produced theatrical productions under the name T.E. Ellis, and made two attempts to establish a national theatre in Wales, both of which were hampered by war – the outbreak of the First World War, and financial difficulties ahead of the Second World War.

From his fortified base he learned the Welsh language, and used his position to promote Welsh culture. He collaborated with composer Joseph Holbrooke on many occasions, notably between 1908 and 1920 when he wrote the libretto for a trilogy of operas based on the *Mabinogion*, beginning with *The Children of Don* and ending with *Bronwen*. The second opera, *Dylan: Son of Wave*, premiered in 1914, and is is believed to have inspired the father of poet Dylan Thomas when naming his son, who was born in the same year.   The castle is now owned by the National Trust, and is surrounded by gardens and parkland.

POWIS CASTLE

Powis Castle was once full of treasures, and many of them still remain on display to this day. It was originally built in the thirteenth century by Welsh prince Gruffydd ap Gwenwynwyn, who was allowed to do so after remaining loyal to the conquering forces of Edward I.

Centuries later, the medieval fortress in Welshpool is where Major-General Robert Clive – aka Clive of India – stashed the loot he collected during his time in India. His son Edward Clive, 1st Earl of Powis, who also worked for the East India Company, set up home there after marrying Henrietta Clive, Countess of Powis, in 1784.

The castle has been in the care of the National Trust since 1952, and contains a large collection of art, including a portrait of Lady Henrietta Herbert by Sir Joshua Reynolds; 'Clive of India's Cat', a Roman marble sculpture though to date from between the first century BC and the second century AD; and the 1660s state bedroom, designed in emulation of Louis XIV's court at Versailles.

The Clive Museum contains an Indian artefacts collection from the Clives' time in India, while the garden retains its authentic eighteenth-century Baroque look.

CASTELL Y BERE

Castell y Bere stands on a rocky hill in a magical location in the shadow of Snowdonia's epic mountain Cadair Idris. Near the village of Llanfihangel-y-Pennant in Gwynedd, the native Welsh castle is thought to have been built by Llywelyn the Great in the early thirteenth century, but fell to Edward I's invading army. Edward expanded upon the original, and began working on a nearby settlement, but the castle was burned down during the revolt of Madog ap Llywelyn in 1294.

One of the castle's towers is designed in the Welsh apsidal style, the stretched 'D' shape which was characteristic of the period. Along with Criccieth Castle, it is one of only two Welsh castles from the period to include decoration in the form of sculptures and tiles. It is now cared for by Cadw.

LLAWHADEN CASTLE

The ruins of Llawhaden Castle can be found in the Pembrokeshire village of of the same name. Looking down on the River Cleddau, a motte-and-bailey fortress is believed to have once occupied the site, but it was rebuilt as a fortified palace between the twelfth and fourteenth centuries by the all-powerful bishops from St David's. As well as being a protective military fortress, it served as a residence and a base for administrative tasks.

The Cadw property retains many original features, such as the mighty two-towered gatehouse, along with the ruins of buildings such as the chapel and prison.

PEMBROKE CASTLE

Pembroke Castle is a gigantic oval Grade I listed castle in the town of Pembroke. Owned by a private charitable trust, it sealed its place in British history in 1457 as the birthplace of the first Tudor king of England, Henry VII. More specifically, he is said to been born in what is now called the 'Henry VII Tower'.

The medieval fortress stands in a strategic spot by Pembroke River overlooking Milford Haven, and can trace its origins back to the late eleventh century when the first castle was built by Anglo-Norman aristocrat Arnulf de Montgomery. In the twelfth century it was rebuilt in stone under new owner William Marshal, who added much of what we see today, including the huge fortified domed keep which is around 24m high. The castle was abandoned following a siege during the English Civil War led by Oliver Cromwell, and it wasn't until Victorian times that restoration work began.

Pembroke Castle is said to be the only British castle built on a natural cave, a limestone cave called Wogan Cavern which can be accessed by a spiral staircase.

MANORBIER CASTLE

Manorbier Castle is a Grade I listed Norman castle in the Pembrokeshire village of Manorbier. It stands in a rather unique location on the coast, being within touching distance of the sand dunes.

The chronicler Gerald of Wales was born in Manorbier Castle, which belonged to his father Sir William de Barry, in around 1146. He wrote in his *Journey through Wales* (1191) that 'in all the broad lands of Wales, Manorbier is the most pleasant place by far'.

Founded by the de Barry family in the eleventh century, it was fortified with limestone in the twelfth century. Restored in the late nineteenth century, the castle is nearly rectangular in shape, with a grand great hall and turrets. It is owned privately.

Carew Castle. © *Andrew (Wikimedia, CC BY 2.0)*

CAREW CASTLE

Carew Castle is a Norman castle perched on a limestone ridge overlooking the waters of the Carew inlet in Pembrokeshire. A stone keep was built on the site in the eleventh century by Gerald de Windsor, the castellan of Pembroke Castle for Henry I. But it was his son who expanded it in the twelfth century, and adopted the de Carew (Caeriw) family name after which the castle is named.

Made from limestone from the local area and surrounded by a now-dry moat, the walls and complex which we see today were added in the thirteenth century, drawing inspiration from Edward's castles of the time, with Rhys ap Thomas adding a touch of Tudor luxury in the fifteenth century.

Abandoned in the late seventeenth century, Carew Castle has been restored by the Pembrokeshire Coast National Park, and is also an SSSI thanks to some rare plants and a population of bats.

A neighbouring landmark is Carew Tidal Mill, a corn mill which dates from 1801. Run as a museum, it is said to be the only restored mill of its kind in Wales.

Did You Know ...

Owain ap Cadwgan, a prince of Powys, was said to be so overcome by the beauty of Gerald de Windsor's wife Nest that he scaled the walls of their home in 1109 and abducted her. Gerald had his revenge six years later when he killed Owain in battle.

LAUGHARNE CASTLE

The town of Laugharne has become synonymous with Dylan Thomas, which makes it quite apt that he did indeed write inside Laugharne Castle, in the summer house in the castle's walls. The ancient fortress was practically a neighbour to the celebrated poet, with his boathouse and the castle both sitting on the River Tâf estuary.

Originally established in 1116, it was rebuilt by the de Brian family in the thirteenth century before becoming an Elizabethan manor house in the sixteenth century. A highlight inside the castle is the tower's spiral staircase, which can be climbed to take in views out over the Carmarthenshire countryside. The castle, along with its Victorian gardens, are cared for by Cadw.

LLANSTEFFAN CASTLE

Llansteffan Castle stands tall on a headland near the Carmarthenshire village of Llansteffan. Looking down on the River Tywi, it was built on the site of an Iron Age fort, the remains of which can be seen today. Accessible from one side only, it was rebuilt in stone during the twelfth century by the Normans, who utilised some the prehistoric defences into their own design. It was the scene of many a battle between the Welsh and the English with further modifications being made until the fourteenth century.

Having fallen into a state of disrepair in the fifteenth century, it was awarded to Jasper Tudor, Duke of Bedford, who is thought to have converted its distinctive two-towered gatehouse into living quarters.

The ruins are now cared for by Cadw.

DRYSLWYN CASTLE

Dryslwyn Castle is a home-grown castle built on Welsh soil by a Welsh ruler. Looking down on the Tywi Valley from its rocky vantage point, it dates from the early thirteenth century, when it is believed to have been established by one of Lord Rhys's sons, the princes of Deheubarth. Standing between Carmarthen and Llandeilo, by the end of the century it had almost doubled in size with Lord Rhys's great-grandson Rhys ap Maredudd at the helm, who was executed following a siege by Edward I's troops.

Now a Grade I listed building in the care of Cadw, much of the original walls and many of the features were destroyed in the fifteenth century.

KIDWELLY CASTLE

Kidwelly Castle overlooks the ancient Carmarthenshire town of Kidwelly from high above the River Gwendraeth. The relatively intact castle, which is now owned by Cadw, was built in stone on the site of an existing castle in the thirteenth century. The defensive building was a state-of-the-art fortress, utilising the concentric 'walls within walls' design. Its distinguishing great gatehouse was added in the fifteenth century.

Near the gatehouse is a memorial to Gwenllian, daughter of Gruffydd (Gwenllian ferch Gruffydd), who is known as Wales's 'warrior princess'. During the Great Revolt of 1136 she formed an army to take on the Normans, but died in the conflict. Gerald of Wales recorded that she 'rode forward at the head of an army, like some second Penthesilea, Queen of the Amazons'. And while she might have lost the battle, her patriotic spirit lives on today.

Did You Know ...

A misty Kidwelly Castle made a cameo appearance in the first scene of the film *Monty Python and the Holy Grail* (1975). But blink and you'll miss it – the close ups that follow were shot in Scotland.

Carreg Cennen Castle. © *Nilfanion (Wikimedia, CC BY-SA 4.0)*

CARREG CENNEN CASTLE

One of the many highlights of the Brecon Beacons National Park is Carreg Cennen Castle, which stands on a precipice of limestone by the River Cennen in Trap, just outside Llandeilo. Its name means 'the castle on the rock above Cennen', and its position on the edge of the steep cliffs offered the perfect defence from invaders. Nowadays, it offers some spectacular views of the Carmarthenshire countryside.

Privately owned but cared for by Cadw, it is thought to have been built by Lord Rhys in the twelfth century, and then rebuilt by John Giffard, 1st Baron Giffard, in the following century. He was given the castle by Edward I for his role in the fight at Cilmeri, during which the last native Prince of Wales, Llywelyn ap Gruffudd, was killed.

Its main features include a square court with six towers of varying size and shape, and a great gatehouse with twin towers.

WEOBLEY CASTLE

Weobley Castle is a fortified manor house in the Gower Peninsula cared for by Cadw. Built mainly from rubble masonry for the de la Bere family in the fourteenth century, it offers panoramic views over the marshlands of Llanrhidian, and out towards the Loughor estuary.

Despite being badly damaged during the rebellion of Owain Glyndŵr, many of its original features remain, such as the south-west tower, which is thought to have been a part of an older thirteenth-century building before the Lord of Gower's modifications.

It is far from being the peninsula's only landmark castle: other fortresses in Wales's first AONB include Oxwich Castle, Pennard Castle and Penrice Castle.

OYSTERMOUTH CASTLE

Oystermouth Castle is a twelfth-century Norman fortress which stands in a prime position overlooking Mumbles and Swansea Bay. It was damaged and rebuilt during its first century, but refortified with stone by the wealthy de Breos family in the thirteenth century, who made it into a much more luxurious dwelling. They added a defensive curtain wall for protection and several new rooms, along with the all-important chapel. It is now named Alina's Chapel after Alina de Breos, the daughter

Oystermouth Castle. © *TeleD (Wikimedia, CC0 1.0)*

of Lord Breos, who is believed to have been the driving force behind creating the impressive place of worship.

Falling into ruin over the centuries, it was restored in the first half of the nineteenth century while owned by the Duke of Beaufort, who gifted it to the City and County of Swansea Council in 1927.

A major refurbishment began in 2009, during which what has been described as 'medieval graffiti' dating from the fourteenth century was discovered.

Did You Know ...

Oystermouth Castle is said to have its own ghost, the Lady in White of Oystermouth, who patrols the battlements at night. Some believe that it is the restless spirit of Alina de Breos.

SWANSEA CASTLE

Not a great deal remains of Swansea Castle now, but its Grade I listed ruins form part of one of the city centre's most notable areas. A wooden castle was built on the site in the early twelfth century by Norman nobleman Henry de Beaumont, and the stone castle replaced it in the thirteenth century. Parts of the south side of this 'new castle' are what remain today.

In the early twentieth century, an area of the castle was removed to make way for the newspaper offices of the *South Wales Daily Post*, which is now known as the *South Wales Evening Post* and is based on High Street.

The castle, a Scheduled Ancient Monument, overlooks Castle Square, a public space once known as Castle Gardens, which has a fountain as its focal point with a giant Leaf/Boat sculpture in the water, designed by Amber Hiscott and inspired by the words of Dylan Thomas.

Did You Know ...

Dylan Thomas once worked as a reporter for the *South Wales Daily Post* when it was based in Swansea Castle. Several of the pubs he frequented, as well as the site of the old Kardomah Cafe, are also nearby.

OGMORE CASTLE

Ogmore Castle is a Norman stone fortress which takes its name from the River Ogmore, the east bank of which it sits upon. Just outside the village of Ogmore-by-Sea in Bridgend, it forms part of a trio of castles, with Coity Castle in the community of Coity Higher, and Newcastle Castle on Newcastle Hill in Bridgend.

The ruin's watery location is surrounded by sand dunes, and the stepping stones outside – a Scheduled Ancient Monument in their own right – can be used to cross the water and reach the landmark. But be careful – they can be slippery!

The Grade I listed castle, which is now cared for by Cadw, also has a legendary history, having been gifted to Sir William de Londres in the early twelfth century. De Londres was one of the Twelve Knights of Glamorgan, a group of knights who followed the Norman conqueror Robert Fitzhamon and whose tales were embellished with time.

CYFARTHFA CASTLE

Cyfarthfa Castle was the home of the Crawshay family, one of the most successful industrial families in south Wales, and owners of the nearby Cyfarthfa Ironworks in Merthyr Tydfil. Despite its appearance, it was designed in 1824 purely as a residential property, and built from stone quarried from the local area. The unusual origin of its name is said to have been taken for the Welsh for 'place of barking', because hunting dogs were often heard barking in the area.

It was sold in 1908 when then-owner William Thompson Crawshay opted for a home which wasn't quite as close to the pollution from the works. Now looked after by Merthyr Tydfil County Borough Council, the mansion house contains treasures from the family's past in a museum and art gallery. These include clothing by Welsh celebrity fashion designers Laura Ashley and Julien Macdonald, and paintings from the likes of Penry Williams, who has been dubbed the 'Welsh Turner'.

Other landmarks nearby are the 158 acres which make up the surrounding Cyfarthfa Park, and the Merthyr Tydfil Model Engineering Society's miniature steel railway on the grounds.

Did You Know ...

At their peak, the vast storage cellars at Cyfarthfa Castle are said to have held a whopping 15,000 bottles of wine and spirits.

CAERPHILLY CASTLE

The second-largest castle in Britain after Windsor Castle, Caerphilly Castle is a sprawling medieval fortress covering 30 acres of land.

Synonymous with the town in which it stands, it was built in the late thirteenth century by English nobleman Gilbert de Clare, and is said to be the first concentric castle in Britain, a castle which uses multiple layers for defence. It was further defended by water, with a series of moats, artificial islands and lakes created for protection.

Standing on an island itself, it fell into ruin before being restored by successive Marquesses of Bute, starting with the 1st Marquess, John Stuart, who obtained the castle in 1776. But it was his successors to the title who really went to town on it in the nineteenth and twentieth centuries. In the 1960s, the 5th Marquess, John Crichton-Stuart, put the finishing touches to the restored castle, which included refilling the lakes with water.

The Grade I listed building is now cared for by Cadw.

CARDIFF CASTLE

Cardiff Castle has to be the most noticeable castle in Wales, if for no other reason than its prime location bang in the centre of the capital city. It began life in the eleventh century as a motte-and-bailey castle, before being rebuilt in stone in the twelfth century.

Successive owners added to the fortress, until John Stuart, the 1st Marquesses of Bute, began transforming it into the attraction that we see today in the eighteenth century.

He enlisted the renowned duo of architect Henry Holland and landscape architect Capability Brown to work on the building and the surrounding gardens. Designed in the Georgian style, the mansion did away with many of the long-standing medieval features.

In the Victorian era, the 3rd Marquess, John Crichton-Stuart, also turned to a renowned architect, William Burges, to further rebuild Cardiff Castle in the Gothic revival style. He worked his magic on the interiors, with each room given its own theme, from Italian to Arabian, and lavishly decked out in the finest murals and carvings. It was donated to the city of Cardiff by the 4th Marquess in 1947.

The animal wall which once stood outside is another landmark, and can be read about in the Bute Park section of this book.

CASTELL COCH

Having transformed Cardiff Castle, what does a wealthy Victorian man do next? In the case of John Crichton-Stuart, the 3rd Marquess of Bute, he creates Castell Coch, Wales's iconic fairytale castle which stands tall in the woods above Tongwynlais.

The literal translation of the name is Red Castle, and the Gothic revival castle from the nineteenth century stands on the site of a much older castle of the same name.

The original Norman castle dated from the eleventh century, being rebuilt in stone in the thirteenth century. But much like Cardiff Castle, it wasn't until what little remained fell into the hands of the Marquess of Bute in 1848 that work on the charming creation that we see today began. Once again turning to Victorian architect William Burges, he took inspiration from the ruins to create a summer residence which was intended to complement Cardiff Castle. Burges died following the completion of the exterior, and his instructions were followed for the ornately decorated High Victorian interiors.

Castell Coch. © *Hchc2009 (Wikimedia, CC BY-SA 4.0)*

Did You Know ...

The Marquesses of Bute even added a vineyard just outside Castell Coch, which produced wine until the First World War.

WHITE CASTLE

The White Castle in one of a trio of Monmouthshire castles known as the 'Three Castles'. Along with Skenfrith Castle in Abergavenny and Grosmont Castle in the village of Grosmont, they were all gifted to Hubert de Burgh, 1st Earl of Kent, by King John of England at the start of the thirteenth century. The castles, which are all within 6 miles of each other, would later be passed on to Edmund, the Earl of Lancaster, the son of Henry III of England, and younger brother of Edward I.

Cared for by Cadw, it is known as Castell Gwyn in Welsh, and Llantilio Castle historically, due to its proximity to the village of Llantilio Crossenny. The moated red sandstone castle can trace its roots back to the eleventh century, but was rebuilt and dates mainly from the thirteenth century, which is when it received the whitewashed walls that led to its name.

RAGLAN CASTLE

Raglan Castle, in the Monmouthshire village of Raglan, wasn't built solely to protect – it was built to impress. Something it still does to this day, as one of Wales's most individual and impressive castles. It was also one of the last castles to be built in Britain, which again might have something to do with the fact that luxury and extravagance were just as much a consideration as defence.

The late medieval castle was created from sandstone for Welsh nobleman Sir William ap Thomas in the 1430s, on a site which is believed to have been a hill fort and manor buildings. The next occupant was fellow Welsh nobleman William Herbert, 1st Earl of Pembroke, known as 'Black William', who added a touch of Tudor flair.

For all its comfort, Raglan could still do the trick at times of war. It held its own for two months during a siege during the English Civil War, but much of it was destroyed following the surrender, and the remains are now cared for by Cadw.

Features include the moated great tower, known as 'The Yellow Tower of Gwent', which has one side destroyed. Nearby is the gatehouse, surrounded by hexagonal towers, with the great hall and long gallery inside. A highlight is the remains of the oriel window, which in the sixteenth century would have been a stained glass showpiece bathing the hall in light.

Did You Know …

Rock band Led Zeppelin filmed parts of their video 'The Song Remains the Same' in and around Raglan Castle.

MONMOUTH CASTLE

Monmouth Castle is the birthplace of Henry V, King of England from 1413 until 1422. He was also known as Henry of Monmouth, and entered the world in 1387 in the one of the towers above the castle's gatehouse.

Established in the town of Monmouth by Norman lord William FitzOsbern in the 1060s, the castle stands on a hill with a cliff face on one side overlooking the River Monnow. Originally sharing many features with the nearby 'Three Castles', it was redeveloped over the centuries by its royal occupants, who included Edmund Crouchback, the younger son of Henry III.

The castle is cared for by Cadw. Parts of the old great hall can still be seen, as well as some of the original walls; it is also the regimental headquarters of the Royal Monmouthshire Royal Engineers, who have a museum on the site in the old stables.

CHEPSTOW CASTLE

Chepstow Castle was built in the eleventh century, on a sheer cliff-side drop, by William FitzOsbern in order to secure the border with England. Overlooking the River Wye, it was originally known as Striguil, taking its current name from the Monmouthshire town in the fourteenth century.

The Grade I listed castle has evolved greatly over the centuries, and has been cared for by Cadw since 1984. Its doors are said to be the oldest extant in Europe, made from wood more than 800 years ago. They have been moved from the gateway for preservation, and can be seen in an exhibition at the castle.

Its oldest building, although modified, is the great tower. The great hall, which can be found just through the grand porch, was designed with the intention of impressing its guests, a purpose which it still achieves centuries later.

Remains of the nearby Chepstow Port Wall are also cared for by Cadw, along with the town gate, which was the only entrance or exit to the town, making collecting taxes that little bit easier.

8

SPECTACULAR SPANS

They might have been built for practical reasons, but the bridges in Wales now stand as some of the country's finest creations. There are those which were cutting-edge feats of engineering at their time, others which took several attempts to perfect, and one which became synonymous with a Hollywood acting legend.

From world-leading inventions to legendary tales of the devil, here are some of Wales's most incredible bridges.

MENAI SUSPENSION BRIDGE

The Menai Suspension Bridge was the world's first modern suspension bridge. The Grade I listed landmark provided an invaluable link between the island of Anglesey and Wales's mainland, allowing commuters to travel back and forth along the A5 from Holyhead to London. Along with aiding those making their way across Britain, it was also welcomed by anyone heading to Dublin, with Holyhead being one of the main routes towards Ireland.

In the days before the bridge, the perilous journey across the waters of the Menai Strait was made by ferry – if you were lucky enough to be human, that is. The unfortunate cattle were often forced to cross the waters on foot, having to swim through the deeper parts.

It was the civil engineer Thomas Telford who came to the rescue, designing a bridge which connected the village of Porthaethwy, which would became known as Menai Bridge, to a location near Bangor. With the river's fast-running waters

Menai Bridge. © *Darren Glanville (Wikimedia, CC BY-SA 2.0)*

and high sand banks, he opted for a suspension bridge which would allow ships with tall masts to sail underneath. It opened in January 1826, and has been widened and strengthened over the years.

Many of the original components have been replaced with more durable materials, such as the wooden deck and iron chains which are now made of steel. Its current incarnation is 417m long, 12m wide and 30m high.

Just a mile away is the taller, wider and longer Britannia Bridge, which stands at 461m long, 16m wide and 40m high. Designed by civil engineer Robert Stephenson, it first opened in 1850 to allow for the increased demand in rail travel. But a devastating fire in the 1970s saw it reconstructed with a second tier, later opening for road vehicles in the 1980s. It is decorated with four distinctive lion sculptures by John Thomas, who also worked on such high-profile buildings as Buckingham Palace and the Palace of Westminster.

Did You Know …

The Menai Bridge featured on the back of a British £1 coin minted in 2005. A sought-after item for collectors, it is now worth considerably more than its original face value.

DEVIL'S BRIDGE

The Ceredigion village of Devil's Bridge takes its name from one of Wales's most well-known and mysterious landmarks. Just outside Aberystwyth, its Welsh name Pontarfynach means 'the bridge on the Mynach', and the Devil's Bridge itself crosses the Afon Mynach river. It is not one but three bridges, the arches stacked one above the other. The oldest bridge dates from between 1075 and 1200; the second stone bridge was added in 1753, and the most recent iron bridge in 1901.

Crossing a 90m drop, a set of approximately 600 stone steps named Jacob's Ladder lead down to the original bridge, which was described by George Barrow in his well-read travelogue *Wild Wales* (1854): 'That shadowy, spectral object is the celebrated Devil's Bridge … It is quite inaccessible except to birds and the climbing wicked boys of the neighbourhood.'

According to folklore, the bridge was built by the devil himself, who appeared one day to offer assistance to an old woman whose cow was stranded on the other side. The Horned One agreed to build a bridge across the river on the condition that he would receive the first soul that crossed it. He had not bargained for the trickery of the wise Welsh woman; she threw some food on to the completed bridge, which her dog chased after, leaving Satan with a canine soul for his efforts. Dog lovers will be glad to know that, in some retellings, he declined to take the animal's soul, claiming that he had no use for it.

In the nineteenth century the area was visited by the likes of poet William Wordsworth and painter J.M.W. Turner, and the seventeenth-century coaching inn where George Borrow is said to have stayed is now named the George Borrow Hotel.

Another landmark in the area is Mynach Falls, a 90m drop waterfall which falls in five stages towards the Afon Rheidol river.

Did You Know ...

Devil's Bridge played a starring role in the first episodes of gritty bilingual 'Welsh noir' TV series *Hinterland / Y Gwyll*, which was broadcast in Welsh on S4C, and bilingually on the BBC and Netflix.

CYNGHORDY VIADUCT

Cynghordy Viaduct is a Grade II* listed viaduct which forms part of the picturesque Heart of Wales train line. The stone viaduct has a distinctive curving shape, and is roughly 305m long and 33m high with eighteen rounded arches. It was built from brick and sandstone in the 1860s by Scottish engineer Henry Robertson, who also worked his magic on Chirk Viaduct, which runs alongside Chirk Aqueduct, and Cefn Viaduct in Cefn Mawr in the same decade.

Trains cross the viaduct as they head through the Afon Bran valley, and anyone wishing to stop for a closer look can hop off at Cynghordy railway station in the Carmarthenshire community of Llanfair-ar-y-bryn, which is a request-stop only.

LOUGHOR BRIDGE

The Loughor Bridge – or the 'great divide', as it is playfully known by some local rugby fans – is the road bridge which crosses the River Loughor connecting Llanelli with Swansea. Built in 1923, although a much older bridge once stood on the same spot, the remains of which can be seen on the western side, it also connects the counties of Swansea and Carmarthenshire.

Heading west, it leads to some interesting finds on the roundabouts of Llanelli. First up is the so-called 'cheese grater' sculpture, the 14m Swirl Cone designed by artist Colin Rose. And then there's the 'gateway to the town' on another roundabout, the iconic sosban-topped posts from the Scarlets' former rugby ground Stradey Park, where they claimed a famous 9–3 victory over the All Blacks in 1972.

SWANSEA SAIL BRIDGE

The Swansea Sail Bridge is one of the more modern landmarks in this collection, having been opened with a fireworks party at the turn of the twenty-first century. Also known as the Millennium Bridge, it was completed at a cost of £2.8 million in May 2003, and the launch took place in December when a flutter of snow, and Santa Claus in a boat on the River Tawe, made conditions much more festive. It connects the city with what was then the up-and-coming SA1 development, the former docklands area alongside the established marina, which had been transformed with new buildings.

The curved bridge gained its 'sail bridge' name from its most distinctive feature, a 42m sloping mast which was designed to reflect the area's maritime history.

Now an iconic part of the Swansea skyline, the 142m-long deck is open to pedestrians and cyclists, and is somewhat unique in only being connected by cables along one of its edges.

Did You Know …

It was hoped that Swansea-born Oscar winner Catherine Zeta-Jones would be the guest of honour to officially open the bridge, but she was unable to attend the ceremony.

PORTHKERRY VIADUCT

The sprawling Porthkerry Country Park in the Vale of Glamorgan is home to many natural attractions, from woodlands to fields to a pebble-strewn beach. But its most distinctive man-made attraction is the towering sixteen-arch viaduct, which was originally created to transport coal from the valleys at the end of the nineteenth century.

Standing between Barry and Porthkerry, the Grade II listed bridge was designed by civil engineer Sir James Szlumper and his half-brother William W Szlumper in the 1890s, having been modelled on the Shillamill Viaduct in Tavistock, Devon. Its arches are around 15m in width, with a maximum height of just over 33m. Built during the construction of the Vale of Glamorgan Railway, the Porthkerry Viaduct allowed trains to carry their cargo along the crossing from Bridgend to Barry Dock, and is now used by passenger trains as well.

In the shadow of the viaduct is Porthkerry Country Park's Forest Lodge, a log cabin used for nature-based activities. Other areas of note in the park include the limestone-pebbled seafront, and Cliffwood – Golden Stairs, an SSSI which contains rare plant species and woodland trees.

Y BONT FAWR

When Port Talbot-born Hollywood star Richard Burton returned to his birthplace of Pontrhydyfen in 1953, a series of iconic photographs were taken of him on and around the village's most prominent landmark. Y Bont Fawr, or the Big Bridge, is the name given to the aqueduct which dominates the Afan Valley village. Built in the early nineteenth century to supply water to the waterwheels which powered the blast furnaces in nearby Cwmavon, it is roughly 140m long and 23m high.

The Aqueduct at Pontrhydyfen. © *Sludge G (Flickr, CC BY-SA 2.0)*

The canal has since been filled in and can now be walked and cycled over, and forms a part of the Richard Burton Walking Trail around the town. Burton's birthplace, a privately owned property, can be found below the aqueduct.

Did You Know ...

Richard Burton isn't the only famous person to come from Pontrhydyfen. The small Port Talbot village is also the birthplace of fellow *Zulu* (1964) star Ivor Emmanuel, and international opera soprano Rebecca Evans.

THE OLD BRIDGE

The Old Bridge (Yr Hen Bont) or, to give it its official name, the William Edwards Bridge, is a Grade I listed building and Scheduled Ancient Monument in Pontypridd. Named after its creator, a minister who doubled up as an architect, the arched footbridge spans 43m across the River Taff.

It was completed in 1756, but it took four attempts to perfect. The first bridge was destroyed by debris following a flood; the second was intended to be more robust, but either suffered a similar fate, or caved in on itself; and the third crumbled under its own weight.

Luckily, lessons were learned and the fourth bridge, which stands next to the more recent Victoria Bridge, can be crossed on foot today, and has been painted by the likes of Richard Wilson and J.M.W. Turner.

NEWPORT TRANSPORTER BRIDGE

One of the most distinctive sights in the city of Newport is the Newport Transporter Bridge. Along with the Tees Transporter Bridge in Middlesbrough, it is one of only two transporter bridges still in use in the UK, and one of only three remaining, with the Warrington Transporter Bridge which was closed in 1964.

Newport Transporter Bridge. © *Lewis Hulbert (Wikimedia, CC BY-SA 3.0)*

Owned and cared for by Newport City Council, the Grade I listed bridge on Stephenson Street allows motor vehicles to cross the River Usk and, at times, allows the public to walk across as well – if you can stomach climbing the 277 steps up the 74m towers to get there, that is.

Designed by French engineer Ferdinand Arnodin, who patented the idea of a transporter bridge in 1887, it carries a section of road traffic across the river on a gondola-like platform between its towers, which stand nearly 200m apart.

Other solutions included using ferries to make the journey, but the waters proved to be too treacherous. A standard bridge would have required a long ramp to allow tall boats to sail underneath, and the idea of creating a tunnel was financially unsustainable.

Work began in 1902, and it opened in 1906 primarily to transport workers across the water to the flourishing eastern side, who would otherwise have faced a 4-mile walk to the next nearest crossing.

Since the addition of a new bridge nearby in 2005, the Newport Transporter Bridge's real value now is its heritage appeal. In more recent times, it was closed for a ten-year refurbishment between 1985 and 1995, and has added a visitors' centre on the west bank.

Did You Know …

The Newport Transporter Bridge was opened by Viscount Tredegar, who was given a silver cigar cutter as a gift. It can now be seen in Newport Museum.

THE SEVERN BRIDGE, CHEPSTOW

For many people visiting Wales, their arrival on Welsh soil will be via one of the bridges which cross over the River Severn. Connecting the town of Chepstow in Monmouthshire with the Gloucestershire village of Aust, the Severn Bridge is the original 'gateway' in, or out, of Wales. The motorway suspension bridge, which is nearly a mile long and 136m high, was opened in 1966 by Queen Elizabeth II. It was awarded Grade I status in 1999.

It was a long time in the making; the initial proposal for a bridge to connect the two countries dates back to at least 1824, when the prolific Thomas Telford, who designed previous landmark the Menai Suspension Bridge, was asked to look at improving the mail delivery coach service from London to Wales. But any plans he might have had failed to come to fruition, with attentions instead turning towards the increasingly popular railways. The Severn Railway Bridge was opened in 1879 to allow trains to cross, and was followed soon after by the Severn Tunnel in 1886.

It was the dominance of road vehicles as the main mode of transport in the twentieth century which saw attentions turn back to the idea of a bridge, and after the Second World War things began to gain momentum, with construction beginning in 1961.

In order to recoup some the costs, the government struck upon the idea of charging a toll for crossing, which was initially set at 2*s* 6*d*. The tolls were originally collected on both sides of the bridge, but with time the toll booths were stationed on the English side of the border only. This proved to be the source of many a joke over the years, with visitors travelling from England

The Severn Bridge. © *Jamie Taylor (Wikimedia, CC BY-SA 2.0)*

questioning why they should have to pay to enter Wales, when the Welsh can leave for free. It was announced in 2017 that the toll would be dropped by the end of 2018.

The crossing is made up of four structures which, if heading from Wales towards England, are the Wye Bridge, Beachley Viaduct, Severn Bridge, and the Aust Viaduct. It is the Wye Bridge which crosses the border over the River Wye into England, before the Beachley Viaduct crosses the Beachley peninsula, and on to the Severn Bridge, which is held aloft by cables connecting two supporting towers.

In 1996, the Severn Bridge was joined by the Second Severn Crossing, which was renamed the Prince of Wales Bridge in 2018. Inaugurated by Charles, Prince of Wales, the cable-stayed motorway bridge was built to ease the traffic on the original, and the wider crossing now carries more traffic along the M4 than its predecessor.

Did You Know …

The cables which suspend the deck of the Severn Bridge criss-cross each other in a zigzag design, rather than the conventional vertical design, to help decrease vibration.

9

LIVING IN STYLE

While the castles of Wales might represent some of the finest ruins in the world, and the bridges are incredible feats of engineering, what of the buildings which were created for more luxurious reasons? From stately homes to luscious gardens, there are many grand properties across Wales with colourful histories, and quite a few tales to tell. Some housed the rich and famous, and had grounds where unique plants flourished. Others were more humble dwellings, and inspired some of the country's most creative minds.

In this chapter, we take a look at a selection of domestic landmarks, which have not only been preserved, but in some cases, are now looking better than ever.

IMPRESSIVE HOMES

Plas Newydd, Anglesey
Falling within the boundaries of Anglesey's AONB, Plas Newydd is a Grade I ancestral home and garden on the Menai Strait. With breathtaking views of Snowdonia, the family residence near Llanfairpwllgwyngyll, which dates back to the thirteenth century, was opened to the public when the 7th Marquess of Anglesey gifted it to the National Trust in 1976. Its name translates as 'new hall' or 'new mansion', and surrounding the centrepiece are 169 acres of greenery, 40 of which are dedicated to the gardens.

Plas Newydd, Anglesey. © *Waterborough (Wikimedia, CC BY-SA 3.0)*

Inside, there is a permanent collection of works by artist Rex Whistler, the prodigious English artist who was killed in the Battle of Normandy. It includes the *Claudian Fantasy*, his largest painting measuring 17m wide. Packed with symbolism, it tells a tale of unrequited love.

Plas Newydd also houses a Waterloo military museum, and one of its more unusual artefacts is the 'Anglesey Leg'. Said to be the world's first 'fully articulated prosthetic leg', it was presented to Henry William, the 1st Marquess of Anglesey, after he lost his own while fighting beside the Duke of Wellington.

A more recent military connection was formed in 1949 when the training ship HMS *Conway* moored in the nearby waters. When it was wrecked in 1953, the cadets trained and stayed in Plas Newydd, and a dedicated building erected on the grounds for the trainees is now Conway Centres: Anglesey, a centre for outdoor activities and the arts.

Did You Know …

The nearby Welsh town of Llanfairpwllgwyngyll's more famous name, Llanfairpwllgwyngyllgogerychwyrndrobwllllantysiliogogogoch, is fifty-eight letters long, making it the longest place name in Europe. It is the second-longest in the world, behind New Zealand's eighty-five-letter tongue-twister, Taumatawhakatangihangakoauauotamateaturipukakapikimaungahoronukupokaiwhenuakitanatahu. A popular landmark is the town's railway station, where you can see the full name on the platform signs.

Plas Mawr

Plas Mawr in Conwy is a grand Elizabethan townhouse built by wealthy merchant Robert Wynn in the second half of the sixteenth century. A Scheduled Monument, no expense was spared on the 'grand hall', which combines European Renaissance influences with local Welsh elements in its design. Badges, crests and symbols from the period can be seen in the original plasterwork, including some that bear its creator's initials R.W.

Now cared for by Cadw, the Grade I listed building can also be seen as the home of the visual arts in Wales. When Henry Clarence Whaite and a group of fellow artists set about founding the Royal Cambrian Academy of Art in 1881, they made Plas Mawr their base.

Did You Know …

The presidents of the Royal Cambrian Academy of Art have included some of Wales's best-known artists, including Augustus John and Sir Kyffin Williams.

Hafodunos

For Victorian grandeur, head to Hafodunos, a Gothic revival house near the Conwy village of Llangernyw. Built on the site of a home dating from 1674, it was designed in the 1860s by Sir George Gilbert Scott. The architect is more famous for his work on churches and cathedrals, and the elaborate home certainly has an ecclesiastical feel. It was neglected and was gutted by fire in 2004; the damage has done little to dampen the majestic atmosphere surrounding the Grade I listed building, which is currently being restored.

Its name is said to derive from the legend of St Winifred, whose body was rested there during its time as a monastery en route to the churchyard in Gwytherin for *un nos*, which is Welsh for 'one night'.

There are several other listed places within its grounds, such as the Grade I hall ruins and keeper's cottage.

Plas Teg
Built by Sir John Trevor in the early seventeenth century, Plas Teg is a privately owned Jacobean country house near the village of Pontblyddyn in Flintshire. Standing tall above the surrounding countryside between Wrexham and Mold, its four towers can be seen breaking through the trees as you approach the impressive landmark.

The Grade I listed building, which covers 1,860 square metres, remained in the Trevor family until the twentieth century, but was nearly demolished in 1950, when Cadw stepped in to grant it protected status. It is thanks to antiques dealer Cornelia Bayley, who bought the house in 1986, that the public can now visit the refurbished home at limited times, or join a tour which includes regular ghost-hunting nights. Said to be one of the 'most haunted' places in Wales, its ghostly inhabitants include the area's Grey Lady.

Did You Know …

Pop group Girls Aloud once went ghost hunting in Plas Teg for an episode of *Ghosthunting With…* in 2006, when they investigated with *Most Haunted*'s Yvette Fielding.

Kinmel Hall
Not far from the Conwy town of Abergele is a Victorian mansion house which has been dubbed the 'Welsh Versailles' for its splendour and grandeur. Kinmel Hall near the village of St George has 122 rooms, and sits in 5,000 acres of grounds, with the house itself set in 18 acres of walled gardens.

A home has stood on the spot since the twelfth century, but the current house was designed by prominent English architect William Eden Nesfield for the Hughes family, who were wealthy copper miners, in the second half of the nineteenth century. A family affair, it was the architect's father William Andrews Nesfield who designed the property's Venetian gardens.

It remained in private hands until 1929, after which it had a spell as a health centre until the Second World War saw it being used as a hospital. Now derelict, the property makes a fascinating landmark as it awaits for its moment to shine once more.

Did You Know ...

In the Victorian era, one of Kinmel Hall's many rooms was dedicated purely to ironing newspapers, to avoid getting ink on the readers' hands.

Plas Newydd, Llangollen

Plas Newydd in Llangollen – not to be confused with previous landmark Plas Newydd in Anglesey – was once home to the famous Ladies of Llangollen. Lady Eleanor Butler and Miss Sarah Ponsonby set tongues wagging in Regency society when they eloped to Wales in the late eighteenth century. The two upper-class women from Ireland lived together for more than fifty years in what we would now call a same-sex relationship.

Despite being considered scandalous by some, they became celebrities of sorts, catching the attention of royalty, and welcoming the great and the good to their home as they travelled past Plas Newydd between England and Ireland. They hosted guests day and night, and those who paid a visit ranged from Sir Walter Scott and the Duke of Wellington to Lord Byron and Percy Shelley.

The couple upgraded the property, adding fantasy Gothic adornments and follies, a lot of stained glass and a vast library. A gardener was employed to work on the grounds.

Llangollen Urban District Council obtained the house in 1932; it is a now a museum cared for by Denbighshire County Council. Having been altered by successive owners, it has been restored back to how the ladies would have known it.

A nearby hill called Butler's Hill is named after Eleanor Butler.

Erddig Hall

Erddig Hall is a Grade I listed stately home just outside Wrexham. Above the River Clywedog, it was established by Josiah Edisbury, the High Sheriff of Denbighshire, in 1684. But his plans for the hall were more than a little ambitious, and years later he found himself penniless and the owner of an incomplete home.

London lawyer Sir John Meller came to the rescue, buying the property and debts from Edisbury. He not only completed the building, decking it out in the finest wares, but expanded it further, most significantly with wings on the north and south sides.

It remained in the family through his nephew Simon Yorke, passing through the generations until 1973, when Philip Yorke III handed responsibility over to the National Trust. But there was a condition. He asked that nothing be removed from the property during the restoration, which retains many of the authentic items used by the Yorke family. This includes a large collection of relics – 30,000, in fact – which is the second-largest collection cared for by the National Trust.

After substantial restoration work, Charles, Prince of Wales, officially opened the building in 1977. As well as providing a glimpse back at how the wealthy occupants once lived, it also pays particular attention to the servants, with a remarkable 200 years' worth of portraits and verse recording the lives of those who lived and worked 'downstairs'.

Other buildings on the estate include a saw mill and a stable, while its eighteenth-century walled garden has winding paths, a canal and a pond, and a series of symmetrical flowerbeds. Its rare species include the national plant collection of hedera (ivy).

Llwynywermod

Llwynywermod is an estate with a very regal history. Covering nearly 200 acres of Carmarthenshire country-side, it was bought by the Duchy of Cornwall in November 2006, and is the Welsh residence of Prince Charles and the Duchess of Cornwall.

It lies just outside the village of Myddfai in Llandovery, and its first owner was William Williams, a relation of Henry VIII's second wife, Anne Boleyn. It blossomed in the eighteenth and nineteenth centuries under the Griffies-Williams baronets, but fell into a state of disrepair in later years.

Restored ahead of the current royal purchase, the couple's residence is a former coach house which has been converted into a farmhouse. There is luxury accommodation in the courtyard, which can be stayed in by the public as long as Prince Charles isn't in residence.

Craig-y-Nos Castle

Craig-y-Nos Castle is the fairytale home of nineteenth-century opera superstar Adelina Patti. The world-famous soprano performed for the likes of Abraham Lincoln and Queen Victoria (who, it is said, came out of mourning for Prince Albert just to see and hear what all the fuss was about).

When Patti first laid eyes on the secluded spot in the upper Swansea Valley it was love at first sight. And having a world-famous singer living there did much to improve the fortunes of the area – even the rail line was created simply to ferry guests to her new home.

Craig-y-Nos Castle. © *Dawnswraig (Wikimedia, CC BY-SA 4.0)*

The main building dates from the 1840s, but it was the arrival of Patti in 1878 which saw it transformed into an extravagant Victorian-Gothic country house. New features included her personal theatre, now a Grade I listed opera house, from which she could perform to up to 150 people, and allowing the servants to listen from an upper viewing area.

Craig-y-Nos Castle is now open as a hotel, with weddings and ghost hunts a speciality.

Did You Know ...

Patti donated her exotic winter garden to the people of Swansea, which now stands on the seafront as the Patti Pavilion. She also officially opened Swansea Grand Theatre, and a plaque can be found in the auditorium commemorating the occasion.

Old Beaupre Castle

Old Beaupre Castle is a fortified manor house in the Vale of Glamorgan community of Llanfair. It dates from the start of the fourteenth century; Sir Rhys Mansel began remodelling it in the sixteenth century, but it was the Basset family who added the most impressive feature, the spectacular carved three-storey Renaissance porch and outer gatehouse. The colour of this impressive entrance alone helps to set it apart from the rest of the mansion, being a distinctive smooth yellow ashlar stone. Designed by Bridgend craftsman Richard Twrch, it includes the family crest and a series of styles, from varying columns to a Tudor arch.

The Grade I listed medieval building now lies in ruin, and is in the care of Cadw.

Tredegar House

Tredegar House (Tŷ Tredegar) near Newport is a mansion surrounded by Tredegar Park's 90 acres of walled gardens. Parts of the Coedkernew country house date back to the fifteenth century, but the building as we see it today was rebuilt in the seventeenth century in red brick. While its creator is unknown, its design could possibly be the work of renowned Renaissance architect Inigo Jones, as it bears many of his trademark features.

For five centuries it was the home of the Morgan family who became the Lords Tredegar, an influential Welsh family who rubbed shoulders with high society. They welcomed visitors ranging from Charles I in the sixteenth century to master of the black arts Aleister Crowley in the twentieth, during the time of Evan Morgan, 2nd Viscount Tredegar. A man who liked to live life to the full, he was famous, or infamous, for his over-the-top parties, and kept his own private menagerie, which included a crocodile and a boxing kangaroo.

The house was sold soon after his death in 1949, and since 2011 the Grade I listed building and its eighteenth-century landscapes have been in the care of the National Trust.

Did You Know ...

The seventeenth century Welsh pirate Captain Morgan was related to the Morgans of Tredegar.

Clytha Estate

Clytha Estate outside Abergavenny in Monmouthshire contains a Grade I listed house and folly in its eighteenth-century landscaped grounds. Clytha House started life as a Georgian mansion, but was rebuilt in the neoclassical Greek style in the nineteenth century. The house's most striking feature is the entrance hall, where Tuscan order pillars support an extravagant concave ceiling.

Overlooking the estate is Clytha Castle on Clytha Hill, a 'Strawberry Hill Gothick' folly. It was designed by John Davenport for William Jones in memory of his wife, and a dedication to her can be seen on a tablet in the wall. Now cared for by the Landmark Trust, it has been described as the 'Taj Mahal of Wales'.

The parkland is cared for by the National Trust, but the house is not generally open to the public.

GARDENS

Plas Cadnant Estate

The 'hidden gardens' at Plas Cadnant in the town of Menai Bridge are said to be one of north Wales's best-kept secrets. The private country estate in Anglesey is home to several Grade II listed buildings, which are centred around a Georgian family home built by John Price, the agent for nearby Plas Newydd's Marquess of Anglesey.

Covering 200 acres, the estate's gardens were originally landscaped in the early nineteenth century, but were left neglected and overgrown until the second half of the twentieth century. Ongoing restoration work began in the 1990s, during which time three distinct gardens have been uncovered: a 2-acre curving walled garden with a pool, a rocky woodland area with its very own nineteenth-century folly, and a 'secret valley garden' with ferns, a river and three waterfalls.

Bodnant Garden

Bodnant Garden in the Conwy Valley is a garden home perfectly located near Tal-y-Cafn, in the town of Colwyn Bay. Sloping towards the mountains of Snowdonia, its 80 acres of gardens were bequeathed to the National Trust in 1949 by the arts-loving Henry McLaren, the 1st Lord Aberconway and grandson of Henry Pochin, an industrial chemist who began work on the area in 1874.

The word Bodnant means 'dwelling by a stream', and the landmark is home to all manner of plants from around the world. It is divided into two distinct gardens. The lower has an air of magic about it as you walk along the tree-covered The Dell to where the River Hiraethlyn flows over a waterfall; the upper has five Italianate terraces, with paths leading off to ponds of lilies.

Bodnant can count five national collections among its rare plants, which are: embothrium, eucryphia, magnolia, rhododendron *forrestii*, and those named after the garden, the Bodnant rhododendron hybrids.

Nearby is the National Beekeeping Centre Wales, which aims to protect the declining number of bees.

Aberglasney Mansion and Gardens

Aberglasney House is a Grade II* listed mansion surrounded by 10 acres of walled gardens in Carmarthenshire's Tywi valley. Dating from the Middle Ages, the house in the community of Llangathen was rebuilt by the Bishop of St David's Anthony Rudd in the early seventeenth century, and was added to by successive owners, notably the lawyer Robert Dyer in the eighteenth century.

It is now a registered charity cared for by the Aberglasney Restoration Trust, and features rare plants in a range of gardens, which include one designed by famed horticulturist Penelope Hobhouse, another inspired by Italy's Garden of Ninfa, a cloister garden which harks back to the thirteenth century, and at its heart, an Elizabethan promenade garden.

Did You Know ...

The recovery and restoration work carried out at the gardens was chronicled in the BBC TV series *Aberglasney: a Garden Lost in Time* (2000).

National Botanic Gardens of Wales

In the River Tywi valley lies one of Carmarthenshire's most popular attractions, the wonderful National Botanic Gardens of Wales, or Gardd Fotaneg Genedlaethol Cymru in Welsh. Covering 568 acres of Llanarthney countryside, the tourist landmark is cared for by a registered charity, which conserves and researches its natural treasures.

Middleton Hall once stood on the grounds. Said to have been an impressive mansion, it was built in the seventeenth century by the family who gave it its name. Extensively rebuilt by Sir William Paxton, who bought the estate and splashed the cash at the end of the seventeenth century, the stately home was destroyed by fire in 1931.

Luckily, another of Paxton's impressive additions still stands today, the Gothic revival folly Paxton's Tower. Created as a tribute to Lord Nelson, it is now a National Trust property.

The area covered by the botanic gardens is owned by Carmarthenshire County Council, and the idea to create a

The Great Glasshouse at the National Botanic Garden of Wales. © *Col Ford and Natasha de Vere (Wikimedia, CC BY 2.0)*

'national garden' – the first in Britain for two centuries – came from pointillist artist William Wilkins. Opened to the public by the Prince of Wales in 2000, some of its attractions include the Great Glasshouse centrepiece, which can be seen for miles around and is said to be the 'world's largest single-span glasshouse'. Built on the site of the old hall, it is roughly 110m long and 60m wide. Inside are plants from around the world, with specimens from as far afield as Chile and the Canary Islands.

Other features include the tropical glasshouse, which was designed by Cardiff-born architect John Belle, and the steamy butterfly house, Plas Pilipala.

Dinefwr Park
The Dinefwr estate near the town of Llandeilo in Carmarthenshire has it all: a castle, a country house, and even some legendary animals in its vast grounds.

At the heart of the National Trust's nature reserve is Newton House, a Grade II* listed Jacobean house built on land which has been occupied by humans for more than two millennia. The house as we see it today dates from the seventeenth century, with Gothic additions made in the middle of the nineteenth century.

Surrounded by a medieval deer park, the grounds were designed by landscape architect Capability Brown. Sharing the greenery with the deer are the rare White Park cattle, who are known to have grazed the area since AD 920. According to the legend, they were a dowry for the Lady of the Lake, who emerged from nearby Llyn y Fan Fach in the Black Mountain.

On a lofty hilltop spot overlooking the River Tywi is Dinefwr Castle, an impressive defensive fortress with two enclosures. Managed by Cadw and owned by the Wildlife Trust of South and West Wales, the Grade I listed medieval castle is said to have been built originally by Rhodri the Great, who was made King of Gwynedd in AD 844, although records date no further back than the twelfth century.

Did You Know ...

St Tyfi's church in Llandyfeisant falls within the grounds of Dinefwr Park, and is often overlooked by visitors. The Grade II listed church is dedicated to St Tyfei, as his name is spelled in Welsh. Built in the Middle Ages but substantially rebuilt in the nineteenth century, it stands on a secluded slope with a burial ground outside.

Singleton Botanical Gardens

Swansea's Singleton Botanical Gardens, in the city's Singleton Park, are home to a vast collection of plants. The park covers 250 acres of land on the former Singleton Estate, and the entrance to its gardens is lined with two long herbaceous borders. Its collections include herb, ornamental and rock gardens, glasshouses, and a Japanese bridge which wouldn't look out of place at the home of Impressionist painter Claude Monet. Its seasonal plants can be seen all year round, but they are at their most impressive in the summer months, with tours and entertainment staged throughout August.

A nearby landmark in the park is the Swiss cottage, which was designed by English architect Peter Frederick Robinson in the early nineteenth century. It has survived vandalism and changing tastes to remain one of the park's unique sights.

Singleton isn't the only garden in Swansea which could be considered as a landmark. Clyne Gardens, a little oasis of calm in nearby Blackpill which is also known for its collections, is home to the Grade II* listed Clyne Castle. Previously owned by the Vivian family, whose estates covered Singleton Park, the stately home hosted the likes of Queen Victoria and Winston Churchill on their visits to Swansea.

Dyffryn Gardens

At the heart of Dyffryn Gardens' estate in the Vale of Glamorgan is Dyffryn House, a property with a history dating back to the seventh century when it was known as the Manor of Worlton, the residency of Bishop Oudaceous of Llandaf.

The current house was rebuilt by wealthy coal-owner John Cory in the late nineteenth century, and has been preserved to maintain the look of the period. Owned by the Vale of Glamorgan council and cared for by the National Trust, it has more than 55 acres of Grade II listed gardens, some of which were designed by Edwardian landscape architect Thomas Mawson. They were commissioned by Cory's third son, Reginald Cory, a keen horticulturalist and 'plant hunter', and retain much of his original vision today. His global voyages in search of exotic plants can also be seen in features such as the Pompeian Garden, where the fountain and columns capture the feel of a trip to the Azurri – albeit with a slightly milder climate.

Cowbridge Physic Garden

A less well-known landmark in the Vale of Glamorgan is Cowbridge Physic Garden. Tucked away behind a stone wall in Church Street in the centre of town, the half-acre garden was once part of the larger eighteenth-century Old Hall Gardens, planned by the local Edmondes family.

Having been allowed to fall into disrepair, it has been revived and is now a haven for plants and herbs with medicinal properties, drawing its inspiration from traditional physic gardens with plants that offer – or at least were thought to offer – healing abilities.

Bute Park and the Animal Wall

The capital city's showpiece park was once part of the grounds of Cardiff Castle. Now very much its own separate landmark, it covers 130 acres of parkland and gardens which are dotted with sculptures and curiosities.

Animal Wall, Cardiff. © *Seth Whales (Wikimedia, public domain)*

The Blackweir Bridge and Cardiff Bridge mark the north and south ends of the park, while the West Lodge Gate at the entrance on Castle Street, and the Park Lodge near the entrance in the north, are both Grade II* listed buildings.

Named after the castle's owner John Crichton-Stuart, the 3rd Marquess of Bute, Castle Green was originally landscaped in the eighteenth century by landscape architect Capability Brown, and later laid by head gardener Andrew Pettigrew in the second half of the nineteenth century.

Just outside the park is the Animal Wall, a series of fifteen sculpted animals which peer over a long stone wall. Originally built outside Cardiff Castle, they were moved to accommodate the widening road.

The Grade I listed structure was designed by William Burges of Castell Coch and Cardiff Castle fame, but it wasn't built until after his death in 1890. It began with nine animal sculptures – a hyena, wolf, apes, seal, bear, lioness, lynx, and two opposing lions – but six more were added in 1931: a pelican, anteater, raccoons, leopard, beaver and vulture.

UNIQUELY WELSH

Cae'r Gors

Cae'r Gors was the home of Welsh-language author Kate Roberts, who has been dubbed Brenhines ein Llên – The Queen of our Literature. Her most famous work is the 1936 novel *Traed mewn Cyffion* (*Feet in Chains*), in which she captured the hardships of life for a slate quarry family in north Wales.

Roberts lived in the Caernarfon village of Rhosgadfan from the age of 4 to 18, and her cottage is now a Grade II listed building cared for by Cadw, which has been restored as a heritage centre along with the garden and the buildings surrounding it.

The Smallest House in Great Britain

The clue is in the name, but the smallest house in Great Britain, or Y Tŷ Lleiaf ym Mhrydain Fawr in Welsh, really does claim to be the smallest house in Great Britain – and the *Guinness Book of Records* agrees.

Also known as the much shorter Quay House, the minuscule abode in the quay in Conwy is bright red in colour, and measures

Smallest House in Great Britain, Conwy. © *Nilfanion (Wikimedia, CC BY-SA 4.0)*

3.05m by 1.8m. Built near Conwy Castle's walls in the sixteenth century, it was occupied until 1900, and even housed a family at one point, until the council decided it was 'unfit for human habitation'. Its final occupant was Robert Jones, a fisherman who, at 6ft 3in tall, had to squat to stand up in his own home. It can now be visited as a tourist attraction.

Tŷ Hyll
Despite the name, Tŷ Hyll – Welsh for Ugly House – is far from ugly. Quite the opposite, in fact. Owned by the Snowdonia Society charity, the home in Betws-y-Coed is said to have been built under the conditions of the Welsh folk tradition of *tŷ un nos*, which means 'one-night house'. According to the old custom, if you could build a house on common land in a single night, and top it off with smoke emerging from the chimney, then you could keep the land on which it was built.

Inside the house nowadays is a tearoom and the Honeybee Room, an educational facility about bees. Outside are 5 acres of gardens and woodland, with a wildlife pond for spotting dragonflies and frogs. There are paths which can be followed to explore the area, and through the trees you can catch a glimpse of the River Llugwy which flows by, and the Moel Siabod mountain.

Yr Ysgwrn
Yr Ysgwrn in the village of Trawsfynydd near Blaenau Ffestiniog was the home of Welsh poet Hedd Wyn. Despite being a pacifist, Ellis Humphrey Evans, a shepherd from the Gwynedd village better known by his bardic name which means Blessed Peace, enlisted for the army during the First World War to spare his younger brother the same fate. But the fledgling poet paid the ultimate price in 1917 during the Battle of Passchendaele, and was posthumously awarded the National Eisteddfod's chair cloaked in a black sheet for his poem 'Yr Arwr' ('The Hero').

The eighteenth-century farmhouse that he called home was bought by the Snowdonia National Park Authority in 2012, and has been transformed into a place of learning and reflection, on the man of words himself, the Welsh bardic and rural traditions, and at the greater loss suffered by Wales and the world during the Great War.

Portmeirion

The entire coastal tourist village of Portmeirion is one giant, and wonderfully eccentric, landmark. The Italian-inspired hamlet in the Gwynedd community of Penrhyndeudraeth was designed and built by architect Sir Clough Williams-Ellis between 1925 and 1975. Its main feature is the Central Piazza, with other areas of note including the Gothic Pavilion and the Bristol Colonnade. But with so many hidden features and secret sculptures dotted across the village, the whole area deserves exploring.

Portmeirion was introduced to the world at large in the 1960s when it played a starring role in the cult TV series *The Prisoner* as The Village. In 2012, the music festival Festival No. 6 was launched in the village. It is named after leading actor Patrick McGoohan's character in the show, who was known only as Number 6.

Portmeirion. © *Paul Lakin (Wikimedia, CC BY 3.0)*

Did You Know ...

The Portmeirion pottery company was co-founded in 1960 by Williams-Ellis's daughter Susan. Despite being based in Stoke-on-Trent, she was already selling her ceramics in the Welsh village when she bought the Staffordshire company and renamed it Portmeirion.

Owain Glyndŵr's Parliament House

After being crowned the last native Welshman to hold the title of Prince of Wales in 1404, Owain Glyndŵr would hold court in a house in the centre of Machynlleth. No. 93 Heol Maengwyn is now a Grade I listed building, and is known as Owain Glyndŵr's Parliament House, or Senedd-dy Owain Glyndŵr in Welsh. It was given to the town and opened to the public in 1912 by Lord Davies of Llandinam. Shortly afterwards, Scottish artist Murray McNeel Caird Urquhart created a large, four-panelled mural for the property, depicting the major events from Glyndŵr's life.

Now called the Canolfan Owain Glyndŵr Centre, it contains a bilingual exhibition and information on the man's life, as well as replicas of costumes, artefacts and letters.

Next to the parliament house is the Owain Glyndŵr Institute, a Grade II listed civic building from 1911 which is also the area's tourist office.

Gregynog Hall

Gregynog Hall is a large country house surrounded by 750 acres of land in the Powys village of Tregynon. It can trace its origins as a home back to the fifteenth century, with the current mansion built in the 1840s by the Sudeley family, who were at the forefront of using concrete in architecture.

Its distinctive black and white colour scheme was based on the local farmhouses, and sat at the heart of an estate which is now a National Nature Reserve.

The house is probably best known for the time spent there by the Davies sisters, Gwendoline and Margaret. The Welsh arts patrons made it a haven for music and art, and donated a large collection of their art to National Museum Wales. They launched the Gregynog Music Festival in 1933, which is the 'oldest extant classical music festival in Wales'.

Llanerchaeron

Sitting on the River Aeron, Llanerchaeron House in the Aeron Valley was designed by the then relatively unknown Englishman called John Nash. The Regency architect, who would go on to create Brighton Pavilion and Buckingham Palace, was tasked with designing the villa just outside Aberaeron in the late eighteenth century.

Owner Colonel William Lewis had a vision of a farm complex which would be entirely self-sufficient, complete with features including a dairy and a brewery. Much of it remains today, as the Grade I listed building near Ciliau Aeron was barely touched by successive owners. In a fortunate twist of fate, it has actually benefited from their lack of interest in improving or altering the premises.

Serving as a time capsule of sorts, the farm buildings are preserved in their original state on what is now a working farm. The National Trust property contains many Welsh animals, including black cattle, rare pigs, and Llanwenog sheep, a domestic breed which originated in Wales. Its walled kitchen gardens contain fruit trees, some of which could be more than 200 years old.

Dylan Thomas Boathouse

The Dylan Thomas Boathouse in Laugharne is the former home of arguably Wales's most famous man of words. The first 'rock star poet', and the second-most quoted British poet after William Shakespeare, was born and raised in Swansea, but later settled in the Carmarthenshire town with his wife and children for the last four years of his life.

The house is set in an idyllic location overlooking the Tâf Estuary, and nearby is a recreation of possibly the most iconic location associated with Thomas, his intimate writing shed. Thomas was buried in the graveyard of St Martin's church, and his final resting place is marked by a simple white cross bearing his name on one side, and the name of his wife Caitlin who lies beside him on the reverse.

Those in search of Dylan Thomas landmarks can also visit his birthplace at No. 5 Cwmdonkin Drive, Swansea, which overlooks Cwmdonkin Park, a constant source of inspiration for the young poet.

Dylan Thomas Boathouse in Laugharne. © *Peter Broster (Wikimedia, CC BY 2.0)*

Kennixton Farmhouse

St Fagan's National History Museum is an open-air museum in Cardiff which houses more than forty reconstructed buildings from across Wales. One of the first to be reassembled, and one of the highlights, is Kennixton Farmhouse, which was donated in 1951. Dating from the seventeenth century, it originally stood in Llangennith, Gower. The Grade II listed building contains features which would have been common in the peninsula in the early 1600s, such as a box bed, which looks like a cupboard from the outside, interior decorations stencilled on the wall, and a wooden staircase leading to an extension upstairs.

The house is a distinctive red in colour, with the original paint containing pigments of ox blood mixed with lime. Some believe this was a superstitious charm to protect the inhabitants from witches.

A part of National Museum Wales's series of museums, St Fagan's is named after the Cardiff village and opened its doors to the public in 1948 with the aim of chronicling Welsh life and culture through the ages. Other buildings to keep an eye out for include St Teilo's church, a medieval parish church from Llandeilo Talybont near Pontarddulais; an authentic tollbooth for collecting money on the road; and even a restored pigsty. It is a 'living museum', and many of the old trades such as blacksmithing and pottery are still practised at the attraction.

Bedwellty House and Park

Bedwellty House in Tredegar has an unusual claim to fame: it is home to a 15-ton block of coal, which was shown at the Great Exhibition in 1851, and has been described as 'the biggest lump of coal in the world'.

The Grade II listed property stands on the bank of the Sirhowy River in Blaenau Gwent, and began life as Plas Bedwellty. The house as it is today was bought and rebuilt in the early nineteenth century by industrialist Samuel Homfray, one of three owners of the Tredegar Iron Company. His son Samuel Homfray Junior continued to develop the area, and by 1839 the house and the park which surrounds it were completed. Following the decline of the iron industry, it was gifted to the local council by Lord Tredegar in 1900, and was opened as a public park.

10

RELIGIOUS MIRACLES

Wales's history, culture and heritage are inextricably intertwined with Christianity. From the grand medieval abbeys to the modest village chapels, religion has been at the heart of Welsh life for centuries. This can be seen in some of its most important buildings, and heard in the songs sung by the traditional choirs which helped define Wales as 'the land of song' in the nineteenth century.

One of the most iconic religious treasures inspired the logo for Cadw, the Welsh government's historic environment service. The Carew Cross, which can be found near Carew Castle in Pembrokeshire, is an ornately decorated eleventh-century Grade I listed Celtic cross, which is thought to commemorate Maredudd ab Edwin, the brother of Hywel ab Edwin, King of Deheubarth.

Many of the religious landmarks suffered greatly during times of war, and Henry VIII's destructive Dissolution of the Monasteries between 1536 and 1541 caused irreparable damage. But thanks to some incredible preservation work, and in some cases pure good fortune, Wales is a land with an abundance of ecclesiastical landmarks.

ABBEYS AND PRIORIES

Penmon Priory
The Anglesey village of Penmon has a spectacular beach, views of Snowdonia, and was the site of a quarry that provided stones for other landmarks in this book. But is is also the home of some religious treasures.

Carew Cross. © *Nilfanion (Wikimedia, CC BY-SA 4.0)*

In the tenth century, St Seiriol's monastery was built from wood just outside Beaumaris, on the site of a sixth-century Celtic priory. Rebuilt in stone in the twelfth century, parts of it still remain at St Seiriol's parish church, which was at the heart of the monastery, and which survived the Dissolution of the Monasteries.

Behind the church is St Seiriol's Well, a holy well said to have miraculous powers. Surrounded by a stone wall, parts of it could date from the sixth century when it is first thought to have been built by the monks.

The Penmon crosses are two intricately carved medieval Celtic stone crosses inside the church, which would have stood outside in the tenth century. The larger is the more weather damaged of the two, and shows scenes that might depict a saint, while the smaller cross is more well preserved and is decorated in the Celtic knot style. Nearby is an Elizabethan dovecote, which would have been used for housing birds.

Valle Crucis Abbey and the Pillar of Eliseg

The last Cistercian abbey to be built in Wales is also one of the best preserved. Valle Crucis Abbey, which means Valley of the Cross and is known as both Abaty Glyn y Groes and Abaty Glyn Egwestl in Welsh, stands in a remote site in Llantysilio, Denbighshire, where a wooden church was originally created at the start of the thirteenth century by Madog ap Gruffydd Maelor, the Lord of Powys who was later buried in the abbey. Having fallen into ruin following the Dissolution of the Monasteries, it is now in the care of Cadw.

The abbey takes its name from the nearby Pillar of Eliseg, a stone with Latin inscriptions erected by Cyngen ap Cadell, king of Powys, in memory of his predecessor and great-grandfather Elisedd ap Gwylog. Elisedd was also known as Elise but not Eliseg, and the inscription and the pillar's name is thought to have been a carver's mistake. While the stone pillar dates from the ninth century, the mound on which it stands is thought to be prehistoric.

Strata Florida Abbey. © *Peter Broster (Wikimedia, CC BY 2.0)*

Strata Florida Abbey

Strata Florida Abbey, just outside Pontrhydfendigaid in Ceredigion, takes its Latin name from the Welsh hamlet of Ystrad Fflur, which means the Valley of Flowers. It was consecrated in 1201, and the Cistercian monks who farmed the area did much to make the giant monastery as accessible as possible, with medieval pilgrims flocking along their newly built bridges and roads.

In the sixteenth century it fell into a state of ruin following the Dissolution of the Monasteries, and it wasn't until the Victorian era that restoration and excavations began.

Now cared for by Cadw, in 1919 it was designated as a Scheduled Ancient Monument, and has its own museum on site. Artefacts inside include some of the original tiles discovered during the excavation, with one, dubbed 'the man with the mirror', showing an illustration of a man appreciating his own reflection.

Outside, the outline of the monastery's original layout can be distinguished, with the best surviving example of its former glory being the western doorway, a Romanesque archway which leads into the abbey church.

Did You Know ...

A graveyard next to the abbey is the final resting place of eleven Welsh princes, including Prince Gruffydd ap Rhys II, as well as one of Wales's – if not the world's – finest poets of the Middle Ages, Dafydd ap Gwilym, who is buried under an ancient yew tree.

St Dogmael's Abbey

St Dogmael's Abbey is a Grade I listed abbey on the River Teifi, and the starting point of the Pembrokeshire Coast Path. In the village of the same name, the grand abbey is maintained by Cadw, and is dedicated to the sixth-century saint St Dogmael, who is said to be the cousin of patron saint St David.

The priory was founded in the twelfth century by Norman invader Robert fitz Martin for a group of twelve Tironensian monks. It continued to expand until the Dissolution of the Monasteries, and remains from this period can be seen among the ruins. Features include original floor tiles, the domestic quarters, a chapter house, and the enhanced accommodation for the abbot and his guests, with the likes of Gerald of Wales among its early visitors.

The abbey's restored coach house is now home to a museum of artefacts from the grounds. These include decorative carved standing stones from the fourth or fifth century. The abbey is famed for its library; its copy of Eusebius's *Church History* from the thirteenth century is now housed in Cambridge's St John's College.

The church next to St Dogmael's Abbey dates from the nineteenth century, but the abbey stands on the site of the church of Llandudoch, which is thought to have pre-dated the eleventh century.

Talley Abbey

The remains of Talley Abbey in the Carmarthenshire village of Talley can been seen from far and wide. Standing in the River Cothi valley at the head of two lakes, the Premonstratensian monastery was founded by the Lord Rhys in the late twelfth century, and after the Dissolution of the Monasteries much of its original stones were used to create new buildings in the village, including the chapel which stands surrounded by a graveyard in the abbey's shadow.

Now in the care of Cadw, much of what remains are foundations only. Its most striking feature is the abbey's surviving tower, which would have formed part of an unfinished church, and offers a glimpse at the ambitious scale of the original project.

Neath Abbey

Once the biggest abbey in Wales, Neath Abbey is a large-scale and complete ruin which is cared for by Cadw. Sharing many similarities with neighbouring Margam Abbey, it was founded as a Cistercian monastery, was later bought by wealthy owners following the Dissolution of the Monasteries, and has made a popular backdrop for the TV cameras.

Founded in 1129 thanks to a large donation of land by Sir Richard de Grenville to the Savigniac monks in Normandy, who later merged with the Cistercian monks, it expanded in the thirteenth and fourteenth centuries before being dissolved.

In the sixteenth century it transformed into an estate with the addition of a large Tudor mansion by the family of new custodian Sir Richard Williams. Williams was a Welsh soldier who flourished in the court of Henry VIII, having been introduced to the ruler by mutual acquaintance Thomas Cromwell.

Neath Abbey would go on to play its part in the Industrial Revolution, with copper smelting and casting taking place in some of its old buildings; it was restored in the twentieth century when it was opened to the public.

Margam Abbey

Margam Abbey in Port Talbot was originally a Cistercian monastery founded in 1147. But the discovery of early Celtic crosses and stones in the area – which can be seen in the nearby Cadw-run Margam Stones Museum – suggests that the land has an even older religious significance.

Its nave is now used as the parish church, while many of its surrounding remains can be visited on the grounds of Margam Country Park. Cared for by Neath Port Talbot County Borough Council, they include Grade I buildings such as the church itself, the undercroft or crypt, and the impressive chapter house in the orangery's gardens.

Slightly further away are the ruins of one of the large outlying buildings, Capel Mair ar y Bryn (the chapel of St Mary on the hill), which overlooks the abbey and can be glimpsed on the hill from afar.

Following the Dissolution of the Monasteries, the land was bought by Sir Rice Mansel, whose descendants married into the wealthy industrial Talbot family. The town itself is named after them, with Port Talbot referring to the docks they built on the River Afan. They also built Margam Castle, another Grade I listed building which stands in the centre of the country park and which, despite the name, is not a castle but rather a stately Victorian country house built in the Gothic revival style. Well preserved and open to the public, it has become a familiar site on the small screen, having been used in many TV shows, from *Doctor Who* to *Most Haunted*.

Did You Know ...

A 'cursed wall' stands in the grounds of Port Talbot steelworks. It was once a part of Margam Abbey, and it is said that a Cistercian monk placed a hex on the wall, claiming that if it ever fell, then so would the town itself. It is now protected by a fence and has been supported by buttresses to ensure that fateful day never arrives.

Llanthony Priory

When it comes to the sublime, you couldn't ask for a more wild and scenic location than Llanthony Priory in the Brecon Beacons National Park. The abbey, off the beaten track in the Monmouthshire village, cuts an impressive figure with its combination of architecture from the Norman and Gothic periods.

Founded in the Vale of Ewyas in the Black Mountains in 1100 by English nobleman Walter de Lacy, by 1118 it was a home for the first Canons Regular who followed the Rule of St Augustine in Wales. It fell into ruin following the rebellion of Owain Glyndŵr and the Dissolution of the Monasteries,

Tintern Abbey. © *Nilfanion (Wikimedia, CC BY-SA 4.0)*

and later attracted the likes of painter J.M.W. Turner to its secluded location.

The ruins of the Grade I listed building are now in the care of Cadw, which also has three further Grade I listed buildings within the priory: Abbey Hotel, St David's Church and Court Farm Barn.

Tintern Abbey

No place in Wales has quite captured the creative imagination like Tintern Abbey. Surrounded by acres of beautiful scenery on the River Wye in Monmouthshire, the abbey was founded in 1131 by nobleman Walter de Clare, the son of a lord whose family kept close ties with both King Henry I of England and later King Stephen. It was another family connection which saw him set about establishing the first Cistercian foundation in Wales by following the lead of his first cousin William Giffard, Bishop of Winchester, who had done the same in England in 1128.

The religious order of monks, known as the White Monks due to the colour of their clothing, were formed with the intention of restoring the simplicity of the Rule of St Benedict – which essentially meant doing nothing but praying and working.

The abbey, as we see it today, is larger in scale and scope thanks to a thirteenth-century restoration carried out by Roger Bigod, 5th Earl of Norfolk. Consecrated in 1301, the new abbey added a touch of the period's Gothic style to the old red sandstone building.

Tintern Abbey saw history come and go, welcoming King Edward II in 1326 and narrowly avoiding a brush with Owain Glyndŵr's uprising in the fifteenth century, until the Dissolution of the Monasteries arrived. The abbey was ransacked, and remained a ruined shell for hundreds of years until the Romantic visitors of the eighteenth century came in search of 'wild Wales'.

Nearby landmark the River Wye became a magnet for many, and was popularised by Reverend William Gilpin in his *Observations on the River Wye, and Several Parts of South Wales, etc. Relative Chiefly to Picturesque Beauty; Made in the Summer of the Year 1770* (1772), in which he describes the abbey thus: 'Such is the beautiful appearance which Tintern-abbey exhibits on the outside, in those parts where we can obtain a nearer view of it. But when we enter it we see it in most perfection.'

The ivy-covered abbey, once a sign of neglect and abandonment, instead took on a much more appealing air in the eyes of those looking for the sublime. Views were captured by popular engravers Samuel and Nathaniel Buck, the Buck Brothers of Buck's Antiquities fame, in 1732, and, most famously, painter J.M.W. Turner. Several poets wrote verses inspired by the abbey, with William Wordsworth composing the poem 'Lines written a few miles above Tintern Abbey' (1798), just above Tintern Abbey. In works of fiction, it was name-dropped by Jane Austen in *Mansfield Park* (1814).

CATHEDRALS

St Asaph Cathedral
St Asaph is the second-smallest city in Wales, just behind fellow cathedral city St David's.

St Asaph Cathedral is the mother church of the Diocese of St Asaph, and today's cathedral dates from the thirteenth century. It was built on the site of the sixth-century church of St Kentigern (Cyndeyrn, who is more commonly known as St Mungo), a Scottish missionary who became the first Bishop of St Asaph. Replaced by a Norman church in the twelfth century, it was badly damaged by fire during Edward I's invasion, and its subsequent rebuild was dedicated to St Asaph, a follower of Kentigern.

Its fortunes waned over the centuries, including another torching during Owain Glyndŵr's rebellion, but saw significant restoration in the nineteenth century by Gothic revival architect Sir George Gilbert Scott.

William Morgan, who is buried in the grounds, was the Bishop of St Asaph between 1601 and 1604. His original Welsh-language Bible is on public display, along with the impressive Translator's Memorial Monument, a Gothic monument in the churchyard which is topped with a crucifix.

Brecon Cathedral

Brecon Cathedral in the Brecon Beacons National Park dates from the eleventh century, although an older Celtic church is thought to have once stood on the site. The cathedral in Powys was built by the conquering Norman lord Bernard of Neufmarché, and was gifted to the monks as a place to establish a priory. Following a Gothic makeover in the early thirteenth century, it became a popular pilgrimage site until the Dissolution of the Monasteries brought an end to its reign.

Restoration began on the Grade I listed building in the nineteenth century, and some of its key features now include the Norman font, ornately decorated with symbols and the largest of its kind in Wales, and its eye-catching stained glass windows which depict the lives of the Welsh saints.

Did You Know …

The colours of the 1st Battalion the 24th Regiment of Foot, who were made famous in the Stanley Baker film *Zulu* (1964) starring Michael Caine and the voice of Richard Burton, have been preserved in perspex cases at Brecon Cathedral.

St David's Cathedral and Bishop's Palace

The faithful have worshipped in the city of St David's daily since the sixth century. It is the smallest city in the UK, based on both size and population, and the cathedral is arguably the most famous ecclesiastical site in Wales, as well as being the country's 'most visited faith heritage site'.

St David's Cathedral was founded on the site where the future patron saint of Wales had established a community of monks. Its position by the sea, on one of Wales's most westerly points, made it an easy target for invaders, and in 1080 Bishop Abraham was murdered during a raid. His grave marker, the beautifully carved Abraham Stone decorated with intricate Celtic symbols, can be seen at the nearby Porth-y-Twr (Tower Gate). The last remaining gatehouse at the Pembrokeshire landmark, the Grade I bell tower houses a permanent exhibition, and also includes the cathedral's bells, which were removed from cathedral's tower in the early eighteenth century.

Work on a new cathedral began in the early twelfth century with Bishop Bernard at the helm. He requested, and received,

St David's Cathedral. © *Hewilson94 (Wikimedia, CC BY-SA 4.0)*

papal privilege from Pope Callixtus II, which made St David's Cathedral a major Western pilgrimage destination. It was said that 'two pilgrimages to St David's is equal to one to Rome, and three pilgrimages to one to Jerusalem'.

As Saint David's cult-like status grew, an even bigger cathedral was needed. It was expanded over the centuries, with additions including the Bishop's Palace, St Mary's College, and the Holy Trinity chapel. But the growth came to a halt during the reign of Oliver Cromwell when it was reduced to ruin.

It wasn't until the late eighteenth century that acclaimed architect John Nash began to restore parts of the cathedral. Sadly, his work did not stand the test of time, and it was up to Sir George Gilbert Scott to give it a total overhaul a century later. Major restoration work in more recent times has included a replacement organ, a modern visitors' centre and new cloisters.

Neighbouring the cathedral is St David's Bishop's Palace, a Grade I ruin cared for by Cadw which can also trace its origins back to the sixth century. What remains of the palace today is primarily the work of Henry de Gower, who was Bishop of St David's between 1328 and 1347. In particular, he added two ranges, a less decorative one in the east for himself, and a grand southern range for wowing guests. The great hall contains one of its finest remaining features, a Gothic wheel window.

Did You Know ...

St David's lost its city status in 1888, but it was restored at the request of Queen Elizabeth II in 1994.

Llandaff Cathedral

Llandaff Cathedral is one of Cardiff's two cathedrals. The building as we see it today dates from the twelfth century, having been extended and renovated in the thirteenth and fourteenth, although a Christian place of worship is thought to have existed on the site from as far back as the sixth century. Medieval and Gothic in style, it suffered badly over the centuries at times of war, from Owain Glyndŵr's rebellion in the fifteenth century, to the roof being destroyed during the blitz in the Second World War.

The damage caused by the Nazis was repaired in the 1950s by the architect and ecclesiastical expert George Pace, who also added the Welch Regiment memorial chapel. At the same time, sculptor Sir Jacob Epstein's prominent figure of Christ in Majesty was installed over the nave.

The cathedral is dedicated to St Peter and St Paul, as well as three Welsh saints whose tombs are all on site: St Dubricius (Dyfrig), St Teilo and St Oudoceus (Euddogwy).

In the centre of Cardiff is Cardiff Metropolitan Cathedral, which was consecrated in 1842 and dedicated to patron saint St David. The centre of Catholicism in Wales, it is another landmark cathedral which suffered severe damage during the Second World War, and was rebuilt in the 1950s.

CHURCHES AND CHAPELS

Rug Chapel and Llangar Old Parish Church
Rug Chapel in Corwen, Denbighshire, might look ordinary enough from the outside, but just wait until you get inside. Spelled Rhug in English, the Grade I listed seventeenth-century chapel has been cared for by Cadw since 1990. The private chapel was created by William Salesbury of Rhug, a Royalist with the colourful nickname 'Old Blue Stockings', with some help from Bishop William Morgan, the man who first translated the Bible into the Welsh language. And he did the opposite of what was expected from a good Puritan at the time: less minimalism, and more grandeur. Grandeur in wood, to be precise, with the chapel decked out in carvings on the benches, the wall panels, the pews and altar rails. The windows were richly coloured in stained glass.

Visits to Rug are often combined with a stop at the nearby Llangar Old Parish Church. Also cared for by Cadw, it is a Scheduled Monument and a Grade I listed building with a whitewashed exterior which again betrays the treasures inside, such as the wall paintings which date from the fifteenth to eighteenth centuries.

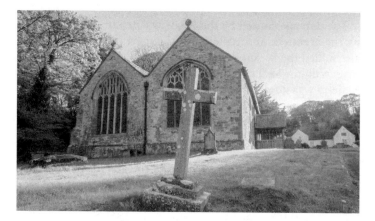

Parish Church of St Dyfnog. © *Jwslubbock (Wikimedia, CC BY-SA 4.0)*

St Dyfnog's Church and Holy Well

The pilgrimage site between Ruthin and Denbigh is where St Dyfnog is said to have lived an austere life in the sixth century. One of his acts of penance included standing in what is now known as the Holy Well in Llanrhaeadr-yng-Nghinmeirch in Denbighshire.

Rectangular in shape, his stone bath can be found in a grove near the church which bears his name, and springs from the surrounding hills fill it with 18in of water.

While it is assumed that a church stood on the site from the time of St Dyfnog, the Grade I listed building dates from the thirteenth century, with its oldest feature being the tower. The main body was created in the fifteenth century, inside of which is an impressive and complete Tree of Jesse window which was installed in 1533 and depicts Jesus' line of descent.

St Mary's Priory Church

St Mary's Priory church in Abergavenny is one of the Welsh churches to be called the 'Westminster Abbey of Wales' due to its vast size. The Monmouthshire place of worship is a Grade I listed building, and along with its impressive structure, is just as well known for what it keeps inside.

The church was founded by the Norman baron Hamelin de Ballon, who would became the first Baron Abergavenny. This title would prove to be beneficial in later centuries when the Tudors' links with the Lords of Abergavenny saw the church avoiding the wholesale destruction which took place during the Dissolution of the Monasteries.

The church is home to many impressive effigies, with its stand-out treasure being the remaining part of a fifteenth-century Tree of Jesse. The reclining figure carved from oak has been described by art historian Andrew Graham-Dixon as the 'only one unarguably great wooden figure' to survive the iconoclasm, which saw works of a religious nature destroyed during the Protestant Reformation. In 2017 it was installed under the newly designed stained glass Jesse Window.

St Melangell's Church

St Melangell's church near the village of Llangynog in Powys has been a site of pilgrimage for centuries. A remote Grade I church tucked away in the Berwyn Mountains, it was founded in the eighth century in dedication to St Melangell, the daughter of the King of Ireland, who left for Wales to live as a hermit. According to the legend, the virgin saint came across Brochwel, Prince of Powys, while he was out hunting a hare with his pack of hounds. The animal hid under her cloak, and the prince was so impressed by her bravery to protect the creature from his snarling dogs that he gifted her the valley to found an area of sanctuary for others in need.

The church is also home to a rather unique religious item – St Melangell's shrine. Said to be 'the oldest Romanesque shrine in Great Britain', the twelfth-century relic was dismantled during the Protestant Reformation and hidden in the church walls. Now reassembled, the monument is on display in the chancel, and bones from the saint are said to be inside.

Church of St Issui

The Church of St Issui in the Black Mountains is a Grade I listed parish church which can trace its roots back to the eleventh century. The restored building in the Powys village of Partrishow as we see it today was mainly built in the fifteenth and sixteenth

Partrishow, St Issui. © *The National Churches Trust (Wikimedia, CC BY 2.0)*

centuries. It is Gothic in style; a feature to look out for is the rood screen, which dates from 1500 and covers the nave with intricate decorations of weaving dragon-like creatures and grape vines.

The church was founded following the murder of the Welsh St Issui, who is remembered in an adjoining shrine chapel. A Grade II listed well became a site of pilgrimage to the saint, and is still visited today. Offerings include money and stones, while a tree next to it is decorated in crosses and rags.

St Mary's Church

St Mary's church in Cardigan, Ceredigion, is another religious landmark which hides some real treasures inside. It stands on the site of Cardigan Priory, a twelfth-century Benedictine priory which sprawled across 200 acres along the River Teifi near Cardigan Castle. The priory closed following the Dissolution of the Monasteries, and has since been converted into a hospital.

Inside the Grade II* listed St Mary's church is a fourteenth-century rose piscina, a basin used during Mass to drain the water; a reredos, an ornamental screen behind the church's fine altar, which is inscribed with the words *Duw Cariad Yw*, Welsh for 'God is Love'; and a figure of Jesus Christ carved from oak.

Chapel of St Non

On the Pembrokeshire coast near St David's is the Chapel of St Non, which is not only dedicated to the patron saint's mother, but is thought to have been his birthplace as well.

According to tradition, St Non was the daughter of Cynyr Ceinfarfog, the ruler of Dyfed who, in an early Arthurian myth, was also the man who raised King Arthur. Her ruined chapel is now a Grade II listed building in the care of Cadw, and is believed to have been built on the site of her former home. The healing water which flows from her holy well, a pilgrimage site where a shrine was erected in 1951, is said to have burst forth after the birth of St David.

St Non's Cross, which can be found in the ruins, is inscribed with a circled Christian cross, and could be an altar stone or a grave marker. A small chapel, known as the 'modern chapel', was built near the shrine in 1934 and is the most westerly chapel in Wales.

Did You Know ...

When Pope Benedict XVI visited Britain in 2010, he used water from the Chapel of St Non's holy well to bless a new mosaic of St David at Westminster Cathedral.

St Govan's Chapel

St Govan (Gofan) was a hermit who made a remote spot on a cliff on the Pembrokeshire coast his home in the sixth century.

A tiny limestone chapel measuring 6.1m by 3.7m was built near his humble abode in the thirteenth century, and can be visited as part of the Pembrokeshire Coast National Park walk. But it involves some tricky navigating – to reach the area near the village of Bosherston, which became a pilgrimage site in the fourteenth century, you'll need to walk down a steep flight of fifty-two steps, the number of which is said to differ depending on if you are walking up or down.

The saint's history is shrouded in legend, and ranges from Govan being a monk who arrived from Ireland, to being Sir Gawain from the Arthurian Knights of the Round Table. He is said to have seeked refuge in the fissure after being attacked by pirates, and remained there as a look-out to warn others of their approach. He is thought to have eaten the fish and drunk the water from two springs close by, and the chapel dedicated to him now stands on the site of one of them. The other spring took on holy qualities, and was considered to have healing properties.

Did You Know ...

The Bell Rock, on the edge of the water, is said to have been St Govan's way of warning the locals of approaching pirates. When it was stolen by the buccaneers, angels returned it to St Govan, and sealed it in a heavy rock to ensure nobody else could take it away.

St Peter's Church
St Peter's church in the town of Carmarthen is described as one of the 'largest parish churches in Wales'. The Grade I church can trace its origins back to the sixth century, when Llandeulyddog was founded in the Roman walls of Moridunum. A Celtic church is known to have been donated to Battle Abbey in around 1110, who passed it on to the Bishop of St David's, and the current church was built in red sandstone and slate in the centuries which followed.

Its key features are its long nave and stand-out tower, which has been more recently whitewashed. It is also home to some fascinating tombs, such as that of Rhys ap Thomas, the man who is claimed to have slain Richard III, his wife Lady Janet, and the restored graves of what are thought to be two of George III's granddaughters, Caroline Prytherch and Catherine Augusta.

St Cenydd's Church
Gower is the place to go for all sorts of landmarks, and there's no shortage of religious landmarks in Britain's first AONB.

The largest of Gower's impressive churches is St Cenydd's church, which dwarfs the picturesque village of Llangennith in the north-west with its large saddleback-roofed tower. A priory was founded on the site by locally born St Cenydd in the sixth century, and parts of the current church date from around the twelfth century when it was rebuilt in stone.

During restoration work in the nineteenth century, a section of a Celtic wheel cross decorated in knotwork was discovered. Dating from the ninth century, it was nicknamed Cenny's or Cenydd's Stone, due to the incorrect assumption that it might have been the saint's gravestone. It has now been set into a niche in the church. A faded effigy of a knight named the Dolly Mare can be found inside, which it is thought to portray a member of the Norman de la Mare family.

Outside is St Cenydd's Holy Well, from which water is said to have sprung after the saint hit the ground with his staff.

A good time to visit the churches and chapels is during the Gower Festival, an annual music festival which takes place in the peninsula's places of worship.

Did You Know ...

The locals are more than happy to remind people of St Cenydd's links with the area, and a panel inside the church is headed with the words 'Local Boy Makes Good'.

Gellionnen Chapel

Gellionnen Chapel stands in a unique spot in the Swansea Valley, and has a special place at the heart of Welsh culture. Built by Protestants in 1692 near an ancient Celtic church called Llan Eithrim in Pontardawe, it was established in a secluded place overlooking Swansea Bay. Now a Grade II* listed building, it began to embrace Unitarianism in the eighteenth century with Reverend Josiah Rees at the helm. A contemporary of notorious Welsh antiquarian and forger Iolo Morganwg, they worked together on studies and manuscripts, and Morganwg is known to have attended the formation of the Welsh Unitarian Society at the chapel, and kept close ties with Rees' family and his successors.

A surviving stone tablet which dates from AD 900 was worked into the wall of the chapel, and nearby was a holy well called Ffynnon Wen.

The chapel now hosts many traditional Welsh folk customs, including late-night plygain services on Christmas Eve, while the horse-skulled Mari Lwyd wassailing custom makes an appearance on New Year's Eve.

Morriston Tabernacle Chapel

Morriston Tabernacle Chapel in Swansea is one of Wales's most copied chapels, having inspired similar-looking buildings across the land. It has been described as both 'the largest, grandest and most expensive chapel built in Wales' and the 'Nonconformist Cathedral of Wales'.

Dating from 1872, the Victorian Grade I listed chapel was designed by architect John Humphrey, with an impressive interior providing seating for up to three thousand people. Large-scale renovation work began at the chapel in 1995, which included a new roof, a restored organ and remastered stonework. In 2016, further improvements saw its tower clock being brought back to working order.

Interior of Tabernacle Chapel, Morriston. © *Matthew Jenkins (Wikimedia, CC BY-SA 4.0)*

Did You Know ...

During his investiture year in 1969, Prince Charles attended a Cymanfa Ganu, a traditional hymn-singing festival, in Morriston Tabernacle Chapel, during which the Massed Choir of South Wales performed. Conducted by Alun John, it combined the voices of the Tabernacle Choir, Morriston Orpheus, New Siloh Choir, Swansea Male Voice Choir, Dunvant Male Voice Choir, Morriston Ladies' Choir, St David's Church Singers and Morriston Aelwyd Choir.

St Cynwyd's Church

St Cynwyd is a church at the heart of one of Wales's most enduring legends. And while the church itself might be considered to be a landmark, what really makes it unique is what lies next to it – the largest private cemetery in Europe.

Just outside Maesteg, the church in the village of Llangynwyd was founded by St Cynwyd in the sixth century, and built in the thirteenth century. It has been restored over time, most notably the work on its square tower, which was given a total overhaul at the end of the nineteenth century.

The Welsh poet Wil Hopcyn (William Hopkin), who hailed from the village, was buried in Llangynwyd in 1741. A character we know very little about, he is credited with writing *The Maid of Cefn Ydfa*, a tragic Romeo and Juliet-style story of his love for Ann Maddocks, a local maid who was forced into an arranged marriage with a wealthier suitor. She is said to have died of a broken heart in Wil's arms. Ann was buried in the church in 1727, while a cross in memory to Wil Hopcyn can be found outside the church.

Llangynwyd is also home to the ruins of Llangynwyd Castle, which was razed to the ground in the thirteenth century.

Did You Know ...

Llangynwyd is one of the places in Wales where you can still see the annual Mari Lwyd Christmastime tradition. A peculiar folk custom, it involves a gang of men who go from door to door brandishing the Mari Lwyd, a hooded animal much like a hobby horse, which is assembled by attaching the skull of a horse, adorned with ribbons and bells, to the end of a pole.

St Illtyd's Church

St Illtyd's church is one of the churches in Wales to be dubbed the 'Westminster Abbey of Wales'. One of the oldest sites of worship in the UK, the Grade I listed building in Llantwit Major is a treasure trove of Celtic curiosities.

Founded by St Illtud, whose name is also spelled Illtyd, around the year AD 508, the complex stands on the site of Cor Tewdws, a Celtic college which dates from around AD 395. Said to be the 'oldest college in the United Kingdom' and the 'oldest college in the world', it was established and named after Roman Emperor Theodosius I, with Tewdws being the Welsh for Theodosius.

Following the departure of the Romans, the college is thought to have been destroyed by pirates from Ireland before being rebuilt by Illtud. The monastic school is said to have had as many as 1,000–2,000 pupils studying there, and counted a few future saints among its ranks. These include St David and St Patrick, although the presence of the Irish patron saint is said to be a invention from a later century. Rebuilt in the thirteenth century, and again in the fifteenth century, it fell into disrepair following the Dissolution of the Monasteries.

Largely unused until the twentieth century, its east chapel, which contains wall paintings from the medieval period, became the parish church. Among the artefacts in the Romanesque west chapel, the oldest part of the church, are effigies of priests and a curfew bell, which would have been rung during the Middle Ages to signal bedtime for the locals.

The long-neglected Galilee Chapel, which was built in the thirteenth century, was reopened in 2013 following a fundraising appeal to restore it to its former glory. Now home to some of the church's must-see treasures, it houses Celtic stones and crosses from the ninth to eleventh centuries, which would have once stood outside in the grounds.

St Cadoc's Church

As well as being an impressive medieval place of worship, St Cadoc's church in Llancarfan near Barry in the Vale of Glamorgan is also a landmark for those who love art and legends.

St Cadoc, or Cadog in English, was a fifth- and sixth-century abbot of a monastery in the village. It was famed for being a place of learning, and he also established similar places as far afield as Cornwall and Scotland. His life was intertwined with myths, and he is even said to have interacted with King Arthur, who he mentions in his own *vita*, or autobiography.

The Grade I listed building has a restored fifteenth-century rood screen and a striking collection of revived medieval wall paintings. Discovered in 2008, they depict themes such as the seven deadly sins and, something of a rarity for Welsh churches, the patron saint of England, St George, and the dragon.

Did You Know ...

In the Welsh Triads, medieval manuscripts which include early references to King Arthur, Cadoc is said to be one of the three keepers of the Holy Grail, along with fellow saints Illtud and Peredur.

HOLY CURIOSITIES

Tŷ Mawr Wybrnant

A sixteenth-century farmhouse in the Conwy Valley is the birthplace of Bishop William Morgan, the first person to translate the Bible into Welsh. The name Tŷ Mawr is a popular Welsh house name which translates as 'big house', although the size of this National Trust house near Betws-y-Coed is comparatively modest.

A copy of Bishop Morgan's original Bible from 1588 can be found inside, along with a collection of Welsh language Bibles and others from around the world.

Did You Know ...

According to legend, a gwiber, a mythological flying serpent, is said to lurk in the area, and might have lent its name to the stream which runs by, Afon Wybrnant.

The Pales Quaker Meeting House

To really get away from it all, head to the secluded Pales Quaker Meeting House, a thatched meeting house which stands on a hill overlooking the Radnor Hills in Powys.

Quakerism took off in Radnorshire in the seventeenth century thanks to three influential visits from its founder, George Fox. The local Quakers were soon in need of a regular meeting place, as well as a burial ground, and the house above the village of Llandegley, which dates from 1717, fitted the bill.

Persecution and the Welsh Revival saw the fortunes of the religion wane with time, until the 1970s when 'Quaker wardens' returned, the roof was rethatched, and the graveyard restored. It remains a place of worship, and is open to visitors.

Caldey Island

Caldey Island in Carmarthen Bay is one of the 'Holy Islands of Britain'. Around 1.5 miles long and a mile wide, it is accessible by boat from Tenby except in the winter months, and is home to a community of Cistercian monks who work and pray on the island. They even make and sell their own produce, such as their trademark Abbot's Kitchen chocolate, and the in-demand lavender Caldey Abbey Perfumes.

Its name in Welsh is Ynys Bŷr, which means Pŷr's island, after the sixth century St Pŷr, an abbot and rather unconventional saint who died after drunkenly falling into a well – or so the legend goes. Its English name is thought to derive from the Vikings, and could mean 'cold island'.

A monastery on the island can be traced back to the sixth century, with the Tironensian monks establishing a priory in the twelfth century. It fell out of use after the Dissolution of the Monasteries, and was rebuilt in 1910 in an Italianate style by Arts and Crafts Movement architect John Coates Carter.

The Monastery, Caldey Island. © *Natalie-S (Wikimedia, CC BY-SA 4.0)*

Landmarks on the island include St Illtyd's thirteenth-century church; the now-automated 17m-tall nineteenth-century lighthouse; and a sixth-century cross inscribed with words from the ancient ogham alphabet. Human bones and other archaeological finds have been discovered in three caves on the island: Nanna's Cave, Potter's Cave and Ogof–yr-Ychen, which means 'ox cave'.

Alongside Caldey Island is St Margaret's Island (Ynys Farged), or Little Caldey Island as it is known. Named after a church which once stood on the island, it now has a bird sanctuary with Wales's largest population of cormorants.

Did You Know ...

Caldey Island has its own currency, called the Dab. It is named after the edible fish found in its waters.

Lamphey Bishop's Palace
In the Middle Ages, when the bishops needed to take a break and get away from it all, they headed for their Pembrokeshire retreat.

St David's College, Lampeter. © *Rhisiart Hincks (Wikimedia, CC BY-SA 3.0)*

Just outside the town of Pembroke, Lamphey Bishop's Palace, which has also been called Lamphey Palace and Lamphey Court, dates from the thirteenth century when it was conceived by canon lawyer and Bishop of St David's Henry de Gower. It had everything that a successful man of the cloth could want: fishing, gardens, orchards, and fields of deer.

It is now a majestic ruin owned by Cadw, with one of the highlights of the Grade I listed building and Scheduled Ancient Monument being the impressive 25m-long great hall.

Lampeter University's St David's Building

Lampeter University has long been famed as a hotbed of theology, and the centrepiece of this historical place of learning is the 'old building' at the heart of the campus.

The university's links with Christianity date back to its foundation as St David's College in 1822, when Thomas Burgess, the Bishop of St David's, identified the need for a higher education facility to train the clergy which was a bit closer to home than Oxford or Cambridge. By 1827, English architect Charles Robert Cockerell had designed St David's Building. Inside the Grade II* listed building, which stands on the grounds of what is now the Lampeter Campus of University of Wales, Trinity Saint David, are the many portraits of those who have helped the university over the years, including Bishop Thomas Burgess himself. It also includes St David's Chapel, which was redesigned by Sir Thomas Graham Jackson, an architect who also worked on London's 'big two' universities.

Did You Know ...

Behind Lampeter University's St David's Building is the motte of what was once Lampeter Castle. The mound is 7.5m high, and while the twelfth-century motte-and-bailey fortress might have been the scene of many a fierce battle between the Welsh and the English, it is now more likely to have students, rather than soldiers, congregating on it.

Our Lady of Penrhys and Ffynnon Fair

A wooden statue in the village of Penrhys, Rhondda Cynon Taf, was considered to be of such religious importance by Thomas Cromwell, the right hand of King Henry VIII, that it was stolen under the cover of darkness in 1538. According to the story, the statue of Our Lady of Penrhys had fallen to the earth from heaven and landed in the branches of an oak tree near a holy well. But it came to a fiery end when it was burned in a mass bonfire of religious images, which also included similar loot from Walsingham and Ipswich.

But you can't keep a good religious effigy down, and a more robust statue of the Virgin Mary holding baby Jesus was erected in its place in 1953. The statue, to which pilgrims still flock along the Cistercian Way, looks down on the village of Llwynypia from the site of the old foundations of Penrhys Chapel.

Just below it is Ffynnon Fair, which translates as Mary's Well. Another centuries-old place of worship, it could date as far back as to pagan times. The well can be found inside a restored pennant sandstone building, built into the hill with benches and a cistern inside. Its miraculous waters are said to be able to cure illness, with Welsh language poet Rhisiart ap Rhys writing in the late fifteenth or early sixteenth century that 'There are rippling waters at the top of the rock ... That can kill pain and fatigue!'

Pontypridd Museum

Pontypridd Museum is an important, and lovingly maintained, religious landmark from Wales's industrial past. Housed in the former Tabernacle Chapel, a converted Welsh Baptist Chapel which was originally built in 1861 on Bridge Street, the museum tells the tale of Pontypridd through the centuries in a series of exhibits. Many of the church's original features can be seen inside, including the still-in-use pipe organ.

One of the exhibitions relates to the history of Welsh chapel culture and nonconformity, including the eighteenth-century Welsh Methodist revival that swept across the land.

The museum stands next to another landmark, the Old Bridge.

Norwegian Church

The Norwegian church in Cardiff was consecrated in the second half of the nineteenth century when the docks of Cardiff Bay were still a bustling seaport. Along with London and Liverpool, it was considered to be one of the UK's three most important ports at the time, and some of the Norwegians who sailed in with timber for the south Wales pits settled in the area.

They included the father of one of Wales's best-known writers, Roald Dahl, who is most famous for his children's books, which include *Charlie and the Chocolate Factory* (1964). Born in Llandaff in 1916, Dahl was baptised in the nearby Norwegian church, where his family worshipped.

Despite its decline in use over the years, its white exterior remained a distinctive landmark in Tiger Bay, and having closed in 1970, has since reopened as a bustling arts centre. Dahl was one of those who fought to raise funds for it, and the Dahl Gallery inside has been named in his honour.

A similar Norwegian church in Swansea's old docks area has also been converted for modern use.

St Martin's Church

St Martin's church in Cwmyoy has an unusual claim to fame – it is said to be the 'most crooked' church in Britain. The wonky Gothic church in the Monmouthshire parish received its distinctive look after being badly shaken during a landslide.

Buttresses and supports have since been added to keep the Grade I listed building safe and upright.

It dates from the twelfth century, but primarily from the thirteenth century as we see it today. In the nave can be found the Cwmyoy Cross; also known as the Cwmyoy Crucifix, this stone cross was carved in the Middle Ages and bears an image of Christ on the cross. It was hidden in the churchyard during the Protestant Reformation for safe keeping.

11

FORGED BY HISTORY

The landscape of Wales has been forged by centuries of human activity. Prehistoric treasures can be found in the remotest of spots, with megaliths, cairns and standing stones feeding the imagination with their ancient secrets. The remains of Roman amphitheatres and settlements hark back to a time when the empire flexed its muscles around the world. And more recently, the Industrial Revolution forever changed the face of the country, beyond recognition in some places, by scarring the land with pits and mines.

From the Celtic tribes to the underground miners, in this final section we'll take a look at some of those landmarks that have a fascinating history to tell.

THE ANCIENT TREASURES OF PRESELI HILLS

For ancient monuments, it doesn't get much better than the sheer quantity and quality on offer in the Preseli Hills in Pembrokeshire. The series of hills – which are also known as the Preseli Mountains, or Mynyddoedd y Preseli in Welsh – are littered with burial chambers, hill forts, stone circles and standing stones.

There are fifteen peaks in the Preseli Hills which are more than 300m high, with Foel Cwmcerwyn being the highest point. The Marilyn is home to an out-of-use quarry, and several cairns.

Most of the hills are part of the Pembrokeshire Coast National Park, and the best way to explore its riches is by walking the roughly 7.5-mile Golden Road, an ancient route which was

Slopes of Carningli; the hamlet of Cilgwyn is in the mid-distance.
© *Dylan Moore (Wikimedia, CC BY-SA 2.0)*

used to travel to and from Ireland. There is prehistoric evidence across the area, which stretches from the Dinas Island peninsula in the west, to the village of Crymych in the east.

The hills could also be the home of the most famous prehistoric monument on the planet: Stonehenge. While opinion varies on where Stonehenge's bluestones originated from, the idea that they could have been transported from the Preseli Hills was put forward by geologist Herbert Henry Thomas in 1923. It was later suggested that they could specifically have been quarried from Carn Menyn, or Butter Rock in English, a craggy series of natural outcrops at the top of the Preseli ridge. There are several other theories as to where they originated, as well as other contenders in the same hills.

An important site which neatly frames Carn Menyn is Gors Fawr's stone circle. Thought to be a ceremonial site, if the stones were indeed taken from Carn Menyn to Stonehenge, then Gors Fawr could mark the route which they followed. Also nearby is Bedd Arthur (Arthur's Grave), a Scheduled Monument in the community of Eglwyswrw which overlooks Carn Menyn.

Thirteen standing stones, along with others that have fallen, form an almost rectangular shape, in the centre of which might have been a burial chamber. If the name is to be believed, it might possibly be the burial chamber of King Arthur himself.

A spectacular site which was almost certainly a burial chamber is Pentre Ifan, Wales's largest neolithic dolmen thought to date from 3500 BC. The chambered tomb is constructed from seven stones, six of them standing, with a trio holding aloft a capstone said to weigh around 16 tons. It is cared for by Cadw, as is the slightly younger neolithic dolmen Carreg Coetan Arthur in Nevern near Newport, which dates from around 3000 BC. It has four upright stones, with a pair of them holding aloft a 4m capstone.

Close at hand is Mynydd Carningli, a 346m high mountain with a large Iron Age hill fort, and the remains of a defensive Bronze Age settlement. Between the mountain and Cardigan is Castell Henllys, which means 'castle of the old court', where roundhouses can be seen in an Iron Age fort, which has been reconstructed on the foundations of an original settlement.

Just outside the village of Maenclochog is the Temple Druid house. Taking its name from the standing stone outside, the Grade II listed property was designed by architect John Nash at the end of the eighteenth century, but was substantially altered in the nineteenth century.

STANDING STONES AND BURIAL GROUNDS

Tre'r Ceiri Hill Fort

The breathtaking Tre'r Ceiri hill fort can be found on the slopes of Yr Eifl mountains in Gwynedd's AONB, the Llŷn Peninsula. The Iron Age fort's name translates as 'town of the giants', and it is thought to date from around 200 BC.

Standing at an elevation of 450m, the relatively intact stone ramparts which surround the ancient monument's 2.5 hectares reach a height of 4m in places, which would have protected the more than 150 now-ruined houses made from stone within.

Bryn Celli Ddu Burial Chamber

Bryn Celli Ddu is a neolithic burial site cared for by Cadw near the village of Llanddaniel Fab in Anglesey. The 'mound in the dark grove', which was once a henge thought to date from around 3000 BC, is a chambered passage tomb surrounded by a ditch and kerbstones. It can be accessed through a stone entrance, with the burial chamber at the end of a long passageway where human bones and other artefacts have been found.

At the back of the chamber an unusual patterned stone was discovered, covered with a snake-like twisting design. A replica is now on show at the site.

The monument has been aligned in such a way to allow the sun to enter the chamber during daybreak on the summer solstice, and might have been used to plot the longest day of the year.

Circle 275 and Druid's Circle

Unlike many of the prehistoric landmarks which are famous for their size, Circle 275 is quite the opposite – it has a good claim for being the smallest stone circle in Britain.

The minuscule attraction near the town of Penmaenmawr in Gwynedd, which has several sites of interest in the area, is made up of just five small stones, which encircle a pit where quartz deposits have been discovered. Its size is put into sharp perspective when you consider that just a few minutes further up the ridge is Druid's Circle, a much more sizeable monument made up of around thirty stones, around thirteen of them standing, spread out over 24m of wild land.

Dating from the neolithic period, possibly around 3000 BC – despite the name, the druids came much later – four of the stones mark a defined entrance into the circle.

The most prominent of the stones is the so-called Stone of Sacrifice on the east side, which has a prominent ledge at the top of it. If the stories of ancient people sacrificing children in the ring are to believed, it has been suggested that they might have been placed in the ridge.

Gop Hill Cairn

Gop Hill Cairn is Wales's largest prehistoric monument. Dating from the neolithic period, it stands 12m high on a hill which overlooks the village of Trelawnyd in Flintshire. Roughly 80m in diameter and made of limestone and stone, its original purpose remains unclear, although some have speculated that it was a burial mound, a place of worship, a defensive structure, or maybe used to observe the stars.

Burial sites can be found in the surrounding area, and there is a suggestion that they could have once formed part of a larger monument.

Capel Garmon

The village of Capel Garmon in Conwy is home to a nearby chambered tomb dating from the third millennium BC. The landmark is considered to be a 'Severn-Cotswold' tomb, sharing similarities with the megalithic tombs from the neolithic period which are distinctive for their length and trapezoid shape. They can be found across Wales and parts of the south-west of England, particularly in the Cotswolds.

In Capel Garmon's tomb, there is a passageway which leads to two round chambers on either side. In the western chamber is the tomb's last standing capstone. The site of the cairn is outlined with rocks, and measures 30m by 15m. The tomb is now in the care of Cadw, and finds at the site include an andiron, or 'firedog', which would have been used for burning wood in the fireplace. It is now a part of National Museum Wales's collection.

Moel Tŷ Uchaf

A cairn circle stands on Moel Tŷ Uchaf, the name of a hill at the bottom of the Berwyn Mountains near the village of Llandrillo in Denbighshire. Its lofty position offers some great views, and is made up of more than forty standing stones covering a diameter of roughly 12m. The short stones, roughly 1m high, are described as 'almost perfect' for their formation.

Slightly off the beaten track, the landmark is just 2 miles away from the Ring of Tyfos, a fourteen-stone ring cairn.

Bryn Cader Faner Ring Cairn

The Bronze Age cairn near Talsarnau in Ardudwy, Gwynedd, is a striking ancient monument, especially when seen at sunset.

Bryn Cader Faner stone circle. © *Talsarnau Times (Wikimedia, CC BY-SA 3.0)*

Dating from around the third millennium BC, it is round in shape with a diameter of nearly 9m, with eighteen distinctive spiky slate pillars sticking out at an angle into the sky. It was disturbed by looters in the nineteenth century, and a hole can still be seen in the centre where the area was unsettled, which could be the site of a grave.

While Bryn Cader Faner might look spectacular, reaching it can be tricky – expect to walk through some boggy land to get there. Some of those who did make the effort to reach the site include Welsh artist Sir Kyffin Williams, who painted it in all its glory.

Dyffryn Ardudwy
The village of Dyffryn Ardudwy near Barmouth in Gwynedd is a place to go to see several prehistoric cromlechs. Its most striking landmark is the Dyffryn Ardudwy burial chamber, a neolithic two-chambered tomb dating from around 3500 to 4000 BC. A Scheduled Ancient Monument cared for by Cadw, the portal dolmen is thought to be one of the oldest of its kind in Britain. It stands in a slab of stones, and would once have been concealed beneath a cairn.

Its position by the sea, and similarities which it shares with similar finds across the ocean in places like Ireland and France, have led some to speculate that it was once part of a larger community.

Garn Goch Hill Fort

Garn Goch Hill, which means red cairn, is home to one of the largest Iron Age hill forts in Wales, and also one of the best examples of prehistoric life in the country. A Scheduled Ancient Monument, a pair of fortified camps stand on a ridge near the village of Bethlehem, not far from the Carmarthenshire town of Llandeilo in the Brecon Beacons National Park, with Y Gaer Fawr (The Big Fort) towering over the much smaller Y Gaer Fach (The Small Fort).

Covering more than 11 hectares, the larger of two has at least six entrances marked by vertical stones leading to a marshy centre, while the smaller fort covers a space of 1.5 hectares. It was thought to have been a bustling hub 2,500 years ago; Bronze Age burial mounds have been found in the area, and the remains of its stone defences can be seen around the site.

Parc Cwm Long Cairn

Parc Cwm long cairn is an early neolithic burial chamber in Coed y Parc Cwm in the Gower Peninsula. Also known as the Parc le Breos burial chamber, the area was a deer park called Parc le Breos in the Middle Ages for the Lords of Gower.

The partially restored tomb was discovered in the second half of the nineteenth century by workers digging for stone, who found the bones of more than forty people. Made primarily from local limestone rocks, it is roughly 22m long and trapezoid in shape, encompassed by a stone wall, and with chambers which would have been accessed by a passageway. While those chambers are now exposed, they are believed to have been originally covered by a capstone or a series of capstones.

Carn Llechart Ring Cairn

Carn Llechart is said to be home to the largest ring cairn in Wales. Just outside Pontardawe in the Swansea Valley, twenty-five stones titling outwards form a 14m circle with an unusual 'crown of thorns' effect. Thought to date from the early Bronze Age, a burial cist in the centre is believed to have been covered by a mound, or it could have been used for ritualistic purposes.

Unusually, the ring cairn has been altered in more recent times by the gas board, who removed the large capstone. In a field nearby, you can see another circle made from larger stones which is much more modern in design – the gas board created it to keep inquisitive cows away from their equipment.

Tinkinswood and St Lythans Burial Chambers

Tinkinswood Burial Chamber is a neolithic dolmen cared for by Cadw near the village of St Nicholas in the Vale of Glamorgan. Famous for its limestone capstone, it is possibly the largest in Europe, measuring 7.3m by 4.3m and weighing as much as 40 tons.

Held aloft by smaller standing stones, it takes its name from what was once a surrounding village, with the remains of more than forty people found inside. The burial chamber would have been covered by a mound, the outline of which can still be seen.

Not far from Tinkinswood is St Lythans burial chamber near the village of St Lythans. Another Cadw-cared for neolithic dolmen, it is thought to date from the same period, and is part of a larger monument which in the past might have looked more like its counterpart. The chambered cairn's capstone, propped up by three mudstones, is 4m in length and 3m wide, and is thought to weigh around 35 tons.

Did You Know …

According to one legend, if you spend the night in Tinkinswood's burial chamber on either St John's Day or the Winter Solstice, one of three things could happen: you could die, you could wake up mad, or – best-case scenario – you could wake up as a poet.

Harold's Stones

Harold's Stones is the collective name given to three standing stones just outside the village of Trellech. A Scheduled Ancient Monument, the trio of monoliths stand in a field in Monmouthshire, and are thought to date from the Bronze Age.

Possibly once part of a larger alignment, they measure 2.7m, 3.7m and 4.6m in height, and their elevated position suggests it was a place of some importance, in line with the sunset or sunrise at midwinter.

They take their name from Harold II, the last Anglo-Saxon king who is said to have slain three native chieftains in the eleventh century. There is also a colourful legend surrounding their creation, in which Jack o' Kent, in one of his many bets with the devil, had a stone-throwing contest from Skirrid.

In the nearby Grade I listed Church of St Nicholas, made primarily from old red sandstone from the area, is a seventeenth-century sundial. Three of its faces illustrate some of the treasures of Trellech: the Tump Turret, the site of a castle which stands on a mound; the Virtuous Well, a holy well and wishing well also known as St Anne's, which is said to be the home of fairies; and Harold's Stones.

ROMAN FORTS

Caer Gybi Roman Fortlet

Caer Gybi is the remains of a Roman fortlet in Holyhead. It is also the town's name in Welsh, Caergybi. Standing in the heart of the largest town in the county of the Isle of Anglesey, the Cadw site is thought to date from the end of the third century, and is notable for being a three-walled Roman fort, with its fourth side facing out towards the ocean waves.

Looking down on the town from Holyhead Mountain is a Roman watchtower, which would have been used to keep an eye out for invaders. In the sixth century a monastery was founded on the site by the Cornish bishop St Cybi, with St Cybi's church still standing today. The saint is said to be buried under Eglwys y Bedd, which means the church of the grave, a fourteenth-century church in the churchyard of St Cybi's.

Din Lligwy Hut Group

Din Lligwy was once a village near the community of Moelfre on the coast of Anglesey. While there is evidence that it might have been in use during the Iron Age, the remains of the stone huts which can be seen today are said to have been occupied by native Britons during the third and fourth centuries.

Archaeologists have uncovered items such as coins and pottery from the time, while the limestone buildings, the foundations of many of which still survive, suggest that it was once a site for working iron. Situated in an elevated position on a hill, one of its more complete parts is the outer wall.

Segontium

Segontium is the remains of a Roman fort outside the town of Caernarfon. It is thought to have taken its name from the Afon Seiont river, and is considered to be the main Roman fort in north Wales. Founded around AD 77 by General Agricola, it could house up to 1,000 military men. But after rebuilding during the second century, its capacity was reduced during the third and fourth centuries. Following Edward I's invasion in the thirteenth century, stones from Segontium were used in the building of the town's World Heritage Site, Caernarfon Castle.

Brecon Gaer Roman Fort

Brecon Gaer, or Y Gaer, is the remains of a Roman fort near the town of Brecon in Powys. Established around AD 75, it was built on a crossroads which linked the south of Wales to mid-Wales along the Roman roads. Originally created to house cavalrymen, complete with wooden stables, the auxiliary fort was rebuilt and solidified in the second century AD by the legion Legio II Augusta. The tombstone of one of the horse-riding soldiers named Candidus is in the collection of the town's Brecknock Museum and Art Gallery.

The fort is now in the care of Cadw, and remaining features include parts of the gatehouses and guard towers, with stone walls reaching as high as 3m.

Caerleon Roman Fortress and Baths

When it comes to Roman landmarks in Wales, or anywhere in the United Kingdom for that matter, they don't come much more impressive than Caerleon's trove of treasures. The three sites of note are the National Museum Wales's National Roman

Amphitheatre at Caerleon. © *Nilfanion (Wikimedia, CC BY-SA 4.0)*

Legion Museum in the town itself, and the Cadw-protected baths and amphitheatre.

Just outside Newport, the site dates from AD 75, and was a major Roman legionary fortress known as Isca which accommodated the likes of Augustus's Second Legion in what was, for the time, luxury. What remains of the bath house can be found in the Roman Baths Museum, where they could exercise and use the open-air swimming pool, the frigidarium (a cold pool) and the tepidarium (a heated room).

For entertainment, there was the impressive amphitheatre, which could have been used for parades and social functions, as well as its more popular use – as an arena where gladiators went to battle, with each other, or with some of the wild animals which could have included wolves and bears. With a potential capacity of 6,000, it was originally built at around the same time as the fortress, but was rebuilt three times before being abandoned in the fourth century.

The oval amphitheatre with eight entrances became known as King Arthur's Round Table in the Middle Ages, where the knights from Arthurian legend are said to have held court. The Round Table itself is not mentioned in any of the ancient texts, and might have originated in Caerleon.

Did You Know …

Archaeologists are still finding new treasures in Caerleon, and as recently as 2011 a Roman harbour was uncovered.

Caerwent
The village of Caerwent in Monmouthshire was founded by the Romans in AD 75 following their victory over the Silures, an important tribe from south Wales. Established as the market town of Venta Silurum, it became the ancient Britons' capital, and housed as many as 3,000 people.

Caerwent's Roman town walls are now considered by some to be the best preserved in Britain. Dating from the second or third century AD, with towers added for protection in the fourth century, they stretch for more than a mile, spanning 44 acres, and as high as 5.2m in places. Cared for by Cadw, the foundations of many of its traditional Roman features, such as the forum, basilica and temple, endure today.

INDUSTRIAL

The Sygun Copper Mine
Now a popular tourist attraction, the Sygun Copper Mine in the Snowdonia National Park was once a fully functioning Victorian copper mine. Work finished underground in 1903, and in the 1980s the Gwynedd mine opened its doors to the public. Just outside Beddgelert, the winding mines, complete with stalagmites and stalactites, can be explored for precious metals. Other highlights in the complex include a large art collection which is rotated in its art gallery.

Dyfi Furnace
Dyfi Furnace is a restored charcoal iron furnace in the Ceredigion hamlet of Furnace. It smelted iron for around fifty years in the second half of the eighteenth century, and after going out of use in the early nineteenth century was later used as a sawmill.

Elements from both of these periods can be seen today at the refurbished site. The flue, which was used for releasing waste produced by the fire, dates from its early days, though its distinctive giant waterwheel is a replacement from its time as a sawmill.

Dyfi Furnace's location on the Afon Einion river was chosen for the power which could be generated from the flowing waters of the waterfall, and the charcoal available from the nearby woods. The iron ore would then be shipped to the Midlands.

Bryntail Lead Mine Buildings

Now in the care of Cadw, Bryntail Lead Mine Buildings are the buildings which remain from a Victorian lead mine near Llanidloes in Powys. Standing in the shadow of Clywedog Reservoir's dam, which was built in the 1960s to regulate the River Severn, mining began in the area in the early eighteenth century. But following a significant discovery of lead ore in the nineteenth century, by the end of the century it was claimed that the area 'produced more lead ore than the rest of the world put together'.

The lead mine had three shafts: Gundy, Murray and Western. It is the Gundy shaft which contains most of the site's scheduled buildings, such as the mill and the ovens.

The Guardian

The Guardian in Abertillery, Blaenau Gwent, is a work of art so epic that it dwarfs the more natural landmarks which surround it. A towering 12.6m-tall miner made from steel ribbons, it commemorates those who lost their lives in the 1960 Six Bells colliery disaster, with their names cut into its 7.4m-high plinth. It was created by sculptor Sebastien Boyesen, whose other works on Welsh soil include Newport's *The Vision of Saint Gwynllyw* and Port Talbot's *Mortal Coil*.

Port Talbot Steelworks

For many, the steelworks in Port Talbot is the defining image of Welsh industry. One of the final bastions of the country's industrial past, it cuts a dramatic figure at night with fire scorching the sky from of its towering blast furnaces.

The Guardian Six Bells mining memorial. © *Tylerian3 (Wikimedia, CC BY-SA 3.0)*

Port Talbot Steelworks. © *Grubb (Wikimedia, public domain)*

Construction began in 1901, with steel production at Margam Iron and Steel Works beginning in the 1920s. By the 1960s it was Wales's single largest employer, with the Abbey Works said to be the largest in Europe at the time. At its peak, it was operated by the Steel Company of Wales, who were integrated into the British Steel Corporation and later the Corus Group, before being sold to the Tata Group in 2007.

While the number of staff employed at the works has decreased significantly since its heyday, it continues to play a major role in the fortunes of the town. Very much a place of work, it is not accessible to the public, and is a landmark which will need to be observed from a distance, perhaps most spectacularly while driving past on the M4 after dark.

Did You Know ...

One of the popular myths surrounding Port Talbot's steelworks is that it inspired Ridley Scott's industrial landscapes in the Harrison Ford film *Blade Runner* (1982). While this has never been confirmed or denied, there is a certain resemblance.

Bryn Nature Reserve

Finally, a true hidden gem to wrap things up with. Off the beaten track, the picturesque village of Bryn in Port Talbot was established in the 1840s for the sole purpose of supplying coal to the ironworks in Cwmavon at the bottom of the hill. The pit's dram became known as Amy, because it was said to resemble Amy Johnson, the first female pilot to fly alone from Britain to Australia, as it travelled up the mountainside.

In recent times, the site of the old coal pit has been transformed into a nature reserve by the locals, who not only wanted to protect the wildlife, but to pay their respects to those who lost their lives during the Industrial Revolution. It is open to the public, and there are standing stones and a picnic area along with an authentic mining dram with a plaque to commemorate the miners who died in the area.

Steeped in industrial heritage and surrounded by mountains, forestry and lakes; with the remains of churches and chapels nearby and a traditional pub and rugby club just a few minutes away, you could say that Bryn Nature Reserve nicely encapsulates all that makes Wales a great country in one pocket-sized Welsh landmark.